CAMBRIDGE

Debussy: *La mer*

CAMBRIDGE MUSIC HANDBOOKS

GENERAL EDITOR Julian Rushton

Cambridge Music Handbooks provide accessible introductions to major musical works, written by the most informed commentators in the field.

With the concert-goer, performer and student in mind, the books present essential information on the historical and musical context, the composition, and the performance and reception history of each work, or group of works, as well as critical discussion of the music.

Other published titles

Debussy: *La mer*

Simon Trezise
Lecturer in Music
Trinity College, Dublin

CAMBRIDGE
UNIVERSITY PRESS

Published by the Press Syndicate of the University of Cambridge
The Pitt Building, Trumpington Street, Cambridge CB2 1RP
40 West 20th Street, New York, NY 10011–4211, USA
10 Stamford Road, Oakleigh, Melbourne 3166, Australia

First published 1994

A catalogue record for this book is available from the British Library

Library of Congress cataloguing in publication data
Trezise, Simon.
Debussy, *La mer* / Simon Trezise.
p. cm. – (Cambridge music handbooks)
Includes bibliographical references (pp. 104–5) and index.
ISBN 0 521 44100 5 (hardback) – ISBN 0 521 44656 2 (paperback).
1. Debussy, Claude, 1862–1918. *La mer*.
I. Title. II. Series.
ML410.D28T7 1994
784.2'1896–dc20 93–42789 CIP MN

ISBN 0 521 44100 5 hardback
ISBN 0 521 44656 2 paperback

Transferred to digital printing 2003

AH

For Debbie

Contents

Contents

Preface

Debussy started work on *La mer* in the summer of 1903 while staying with his parents-in-law in the country. Over two years later the 'three symphonic sketches' were poorly presented by one of Paris's most prestigious orchestral societies to a public seething with indignation at Debussy's marital misdemeanours. This first audience had no inkling it was in the presence of a work that was to acquire, in Edward Lockspeiser's words, 'the appeal and significance for our generation of a work such as the Beethoven Fifth Symphony at . . . the beginning of the century'.

What *La mer* meant to its creator we may never know, for Debussy gave little away in his writings and correspondence. Many emotional and artistic influences may have been caught up in this multi-faceted work, including repercussions of his preoccupation with Poe's *The Fall of the House of Usher* and the emotional turmoil of his flight to Jersey with Emma Bardac, shortly to be his second wife. I have attempted to discuss as many of the artistic, musical, and personal influences on *La mer* as space permitted.

The analytical tasks undertaken in chapters 6 and 7 would probably have had little appeal to Debussy, for whom analysis was a wanton destruction of the mystery that formed the soul and heartbeat of music. When he wrote 'there is at present a strange mania that demands that the music critic explain, take things to pieces, and, to put it bluntly, kill in cold blood all the mystery or even the emotion of a piece' he was probably referring to the fairly modest thematic and formal analyses that were then appearing of his music, and perhaps the early attempts to explain his harmony; he could have had no notion of the lengths to which modern-day analysis would go to explain, or to use a fashionable term, explicate a work or style.

The analytical and critical judgements in this book are my own and should not be regarded as 'mainstream'. This may irritate some readers, but my defence is the absence of maturity in certain aspects of Debussy studies. Although there has been a fair amount of analytical work on Debussy, no consensus has arisen as to how best to do it; one may argue that this is also true of Beethoven and Brahms, but at least agreement exists among analysts concerning the use of Schenker's theories for the study of their tonal procedures. In contrast, Debussy has inspired very individual approaches, including those of Richard S. Parks, who uses set theory (as developed by Allen Forte) for the analysis of Debussy's tonal structures, and Roy Howat, whose *Debussy in Proportion* offers wide-ranging evidence for the presence of Golden Section and other proportional procedures in *La mer*. Neither approach would be accepted wholeheartedly by a majority of Debussy analysts, and they do not appeal greatly to me; hence the need for alternatives. Given the character of this study, it is not appropriate to fight the theoretical battles here, but I will continue to refer to these and other studies of *La mer*.

In pursuing the 'meaning' of *La mer* I have tried not to fall into the trap of believing that analysis by itself can unravel everything. Debussy called for an imaginative involvement on the part of the listener, a willingness to be immersed in a complex but principally pleasurable aesthetic experience. Various '-isms' floating about Paris at this time, especially 'Impressionism', often fail to shed light on this experience, so perhaps it is preferable to administer a stiff sedative to the cult of the '-ism' and accept *La mer* as a work that was both subversive of, and responsive to, Debussy's diverse cultural inheritance.

Acknowledgements

Anyone studying *La mer* owes a considerable debt to the work of Marie Rolf, whose dissertation, inspired by her study of the Sibley manuscript (see chapter 2), was never published. Fortunately, much of her experience will, by the time this handbook appears, have been turned into the critical edition of *La mer* and accompanying documentation in *Œuvres complètes de Debussy*.

I should like to thank Julian Rushton for his support and advice at all stages, Rhona Gouldson for extensive help in preparing the performance table (chapter 3), Barbara Wright for transcribing the literary portion of the notebook quoted in chapter 1 and assisting in its translation (also advising on other translations), Penny Souster of Cambridge University Press for good advice and for supporting the project, Hormoz Farhat (Professor of Music, Trinity College, Dublin), who arranged a Michaelmas sabbatical for me in 1992, Philip McEvansoneya for advising on artistic matters, Julian Rushton, Debbie Metrustry, and my father for reading over the manuscript (and both my parents for everything), Craig Ayrey, Denis Herlin, Roy Howat, Richard

Langham Smith, Marie Rolf, the Bibliothèque Nationale (Paris), and Top Type Music Bureau (Dublin) for setting the music examples.

Note on editions and references

La mer was published in full score in 1905 by Durand. This score (and the miniature photographically reproduced from it) remains in circulation, as do the 1905 orchestral parts. Four years later, in 1909, Durand published a second edition of the orchestral score with corrections and revisions (Debussy's second thoughts will be discussed in chapter 2). It would be pleasing to report that the second edition provided us with a definitive text prepared under Debussy's supervision, but there are still numerous mistakes and inconsistencies, plus a few ambiguities that puzzle interpreters (a new edition in 1938 based on the 1905 plates further confused matters and may be partly responsible for the problems in the Eulenburg and Peters editions). Unless there is an opportunity to consult the new score in the *Œuvres complètes de Debussy*, which is as close to a definitive version as we are likely to get, the 1909 Durand score will be, for most readers, the best available version of the work. Dover (1983), Kalmus, and the International Music Company have published offprints of this that are widely and cheaply available; they contain no additions other than helpful ones, such as Italian equivalents of French tempo markings. The Eulenburg score (1969) is a feeble publication that arbitrarily mixes the Durand editions, retains the inaccuracies of both, adds a few more, and obscures Debussy's intentions by supplying otiose phrase marks, several of which alter the meaning of a line. Even more disastrous is the Peters score (1972), edited by Max Pommer, which has the appearance of a critical edition, but also mixes editions, while adding or distorting phrase marks (the trumpet/horn fanfares in the third movement are correctly omitted in line with the 1909 revision, but the high cornet parts of 1905 in bars 286–9 are retained by both Eulenburg and Peters). For extensive discussion and comparison of editions see Rolf, 'Debussy's *La mer*'.

Bar numbers are not provided in the Durand score or its offprints, so a separate sequence for each movement should ideally be supplied by the reader (rehearsal cues are thinly spread and would involve too much counting back and forth to be helpful as a system of reference here). I will generally refer to bar numbers as, for example, 'III/2', which denotes bar 2 of the third movement.

A score, a good recording or two (see chapter 3), and a little patience are all the reader needs to make the most of chapters 6 and 7. I have assumed knowledge of terms like 'sonata form', 'dominant seventh', and 'upbeat' in the these chapters, but not of theoretical systems such as Schenker's or Forte's. Given the radical nature of Debussy's music, this involved less self-sacrifice than one might have expected.

Piano arrangements

After sending the manuscript full score to his publisher in 1905, Debussy started work on the piano-duet version, four hands at one instrument (now reprinted by Dover). This was published around the time of the orchestral score and reflects the manuscript full score in many of its details: for example, the first source to indicate a gradual *accelerando* through the Franckian theme in 'Dialogue du vent et de la mer' (III/56–71) is the 1905 edition of the orchestral score; neither the manuscript full score nor the piano-duet arrangement includes this apparently last-minute addition. No revision of Debussy's piano-duet arrangement was undertaken.

André Caplet made an arrangement for six hands at two pianos which was played on 6 March 1908 (unpublished); his four-handed arrangement for two pianos was published (Durand, 1909). Lucien Garban's excellent solo-piano version (Durand, 1938) appears to have been based on the 1938 Durand full score.

1

Debussy: 1903-1905

Life

The sea's influence seems to have been with Debussy from his earliest years, for references to it recur like a leitmotif through his correspondence and writings. In 1889, as a young man a few years away from his first great successes, he was asked in a questionnaire what he would like to be if not himself, to which he replied, 'a sailor'.[1] René Peter, a friend, recounted this colourful portrait of the composer during a sea trip from St Lunaire to Cancale, described here by Keith Spence:

> To get to Cancale by sea you have to round the dangerous headland of the Pointe de Grouin into the Bay of Mont St Michel, and the party was presumably at about this stage of the voyage (20 minutes from Cancale, says Peter), and feeling thoroughly miserable . . . A storm was getting up, and the boatowner and his mate were grumbling. First Germaine was sick, then the other passengers, except for Debussy and René himself. There was a cloudburst overhead, and in the midst of freezing rain the boat danced up and down 'like a porpoise'. Debussy was thoroughly enjoying himself, but the boatman got furious and accused him of risking all their lives for the sake of 'sensations fortes'. To which Debussy replied: 'There is one powerful sensation I have never experienced, the sensation of danger! It is not unpleasant. You are alive!'

They recovered and had lunch in Cancale, after which all but Debussy went for a walk. When the friends got back to take the carriage home to St Lunaire, they found a note from him that read, 'I have been smitten not with seasickness, but with sea-seeing-sickness'. It was several days before they saw him again.[2]

Water had featured in Debussy's music before *La mer* in 'En bateau' (*Petite suite*, 1888–9), 'Le jet d'eau' (*Cinq poèmes de Baudelaire*, 1889), 'La mer est plus belle' (*Trois mélodies*, 1891), 'De grève' (*Proses lyriques*, 1892), 'Sirènes' (*Nocturnes*, 1897–9), 'Jardins sous la pluie' (*Estampes*, 1903), and *L'isle joyeuse* (1904); the tranquil 'Reflets dans l'eau' (*Images* I, 1904–5) was completed after *La mer*, so prompting Dietschy to reflect that 'If *La mer* can be said to contain the sentimental storm that then beset Debussy, "Reflets dans l'eau" can be said to mark its conclusion.'[3] Nature had spoken to him and he allowed his emotional world to be absorbed in his response; he wrote:

Who can know the secret of musical composition? The sound of the sea, the outline of a horizon, the wind in the leaves, the cry of a bird – these set off complex impressions in us. And suddenly, without the consent of anyone on this earth, one of these memories bursts forth, expressing itself in the language of music. It carries its own harmony within itself.[4]

It is not surprising that one of the most impressionable and turbulent periods in his life should have produced *L'isle joyeuse* and *La mer*, his most consummate responses to the sea.

Before considering Debussy's private circumstances at the time he began *La mer*, we should consider the state of his career. He was, as ever, in severe financial straits; his was a Bohemian existence that took sustenance when it was offered, and would rather spend the house-keeping on oriental trinkets than food. Although on the surface his life may have seemed to preserve the shadowy existence of the early years, in the musical world of Paris and beyond, Debussy had long been a semi-establishment figure, and he was now becoming a *cause célèbre* thanks to the astonishing success of *Pelléas et Mélisande* in 1902 (première at the Opéra Comique). Since 1888 he had been an active member of the respectable Société Nationale alongside the very man so often cited as his antipode, Vincent d'Indy (with whom he generally enjoyed cordial relations). The Société had been skilfully wooed by Debussy, and it was instrumental in arranging many first performances for him; in return, Debussy served on its committee in 1893–4 and later years.[5] Connoisseurs had recognised in the *Prélude à l'après-midi d'un faune* (1892–4) a masterpiece of French music, a triumphant musical incarnation of contemporary intellectual currents, but it took a success in the opera house – still the greatest prize of all – to set in train a movement that revolted the composer, Debussyism. In 1903 the Debussyists were only just getting into their stride; within a few years Charles Francis Caillard and José de Bérys published their infamous *Le cas Debussy* (Paris, 1910); the retiring man at the centre of it all had become coffee-table gossip.

The period of composition spans a time of upheaval and renewal in Debussy's personal life, but when he began *La mer* he appeared still happily married to 'Lilly' *née* Rosalie Texier (they married on 19 October 1899). In August 1903, when we first hear of the composition of *La mer*, Debussy was staying with his parents-in-law at Bichain par Villeneuve-la-Guyard, where he was with his 'little wife'. He seems to have been happy enough there, taking long walks in the country and visiting nearby beauty spots, including the cathedral at Sens.[6]

Returning to Paris on 1 October 1903, Debussy met Emma Bardac (*née* Moyse) for the first time. They continued to meet, often at Lilly's insistence (little did she know!). She was 'small, stylish, youthful in appearance, open to all emotions, simple, forthright' exuding 'an insinuating charm to which all sorts of men were responsive', including Fauré, who had been intimately associated with her; he wrote *La bonne chanson* (1892–4) for her.[7]

On 16 July 1904 Debussy wrote to Lilly in an intimate, apparently loverly way after receiving a telegram from her, which he described as 'an extra dish . . . and the nicest of all'. He apologises for putting her 'deliberately on the train', and wishes her to understand that he thinks he has 'found a new path', which he dare not abandon, 'whatever the cost'. He begs her not to be resentful. There is also a potentially barbed reference to his need to support her in the manner to which she has become accustomed.[8] After the break-up of their marriage, and possibly in preparation for the ensuing litigation, he jotted down a private record (in a notebook) of the events surrounding this trying time, hitherto little known, in which he criticises Lilly for her dissimulation and profligacy.[9] The July letter, then, would have been a disturbing missive for Lilly, difficult to decode. In the same month, what had been darkly hinted at in the letter became painfully clear to Lilly: Debussy fled to Jersey with Emma. The letter was, it seems, an ingenious farewell. What makes Debussy's conduct seem duplicitous is the letter he wrote to Emma on Thursday [9 June 1904] requesting, 'with true feeling', a private talk. This is a sign that things were getting serious between them well over a month before their flight to Jersey when Debussy was still signing his letters to Lilly, 'Yours passionately, tenderly'.[10]

In May 1904 Debussy recorded five of his *Ariettes oubliées* and a single excerpt from *Pelléas* with his first and favourite Mélisande, Mary Garden, a friend of Lilly. She recalled that in June of that year Debussy had declared his love for her! She turned him down; having no feelings for Debussy as a man, she also felt that he was more in love with her Mélisande than her womanhood. If her testimony is reliable and the date correct – both are disputed – Debussy's state of mind in 1904 must, to say the least, have been confused (Garden mistakenly places the consolidation of his relationship with Emma in September, some months after his declaration to her).[11]

Debussy saw Lilly's attempted suicide on 13 October 1904 as a staged event, for on his way to Dieppe he received a suicide note, possibly one of four (see below), that was apparently intended to reach him after the event. He rushed back to their home in the rue Cardinet to find her wounded but fully conscious on the floor. In spite of the request that she be allowed to die unless he returned to her, Debussy summoned an ambulance – his last husbandly act. She finally entered a private clinic at 33, rue Blanche.[12] Garden describes a visit to her:

They took me into a tiny room, and there lay Lilly, with a bullet in her breast, wanting to die because her Claude had not come back to her . . . lying underneath Lilly's left breast was a round dark hole where the bullet had gone in, without touching anything vital – and Lilly didn't die. They never got the bullet out. That little token of her love for Claude Debussy stayed with her till she died.[13]

Lilly's action merely reinforced Debussy's bitterness. Several friends deserted him, perhaps believing that he was as attracted to the Bardac fortune as to Emma. His resentment was such that he scribbled down a ferocious attack upon Lilly and his friends, then, wondering at the vehemence of it, modified its language slightly, while leaving no doubt as to its import: 'If Madame D had not been a whore had been an honest woman, it is probable that my friends would not have supported her so much. !!'[14] I have not found other direct references to Lilly's possible infidelity; perhaps the situation was so intolerable that he wrote down the first thing that came to mind. On the other hand, he took the trouble to change the wording and inscribed two large exclamation marks underneath.

A few weeks later, when he made the record of these traumatic events in the notebook, the news of her suicide attempt had reached *Le Figaro*, and Debussy's misdemeanours were public property. The most informative parts of the notebook are transcribed below. Some entries are bizarre, others cryptic; all of them give a unique glimpse of his state of mind at the time he was working on the last two movements of *La mer*; apart from some letters to Lilly recently brought to light, there is little else in his literary legacy to compare with this:[15]

On telephoning rue Blanche for news, it was never in accord with the news given to my father.

Madame D[ebussy] claimed that she wanted to allow herself to die from hunger. The maid, who never left her, claims that she took four egg yolks per day in tea.

The maid, who did not want to die of hunger, was only allowed one egg at each meal.

Suicide attempt on 13 October – with four warning letters – nothing in the newspapers until 3 November.

4

The partial [*illegible*] patient, but she was able to make visits ten days later.

Claims that I belittled rue Blanche. There is not a word of truth in that.

I never sought a medico-legal intervention, thinking that she would have nothing to assert in relation to past deeds, which *I* alone can tell, having had to bear them alone, and that a feature of Madame D is never to say or show anything in front of strangers.

Anger – even in front of her own people – violence towards the servants.

Disputes over money, although I had left her more than I could afford (debts) – the subject of bitter reproaches.

Lies of all kinds, saying that my part in it was slight.

Constant dissimulations. For example, has never loved me – has never sought anything other than an improved position. Moreover she was always wrong and avenged herself in exercising a daily tyranny on my thoughts, my contacts – the material proof of this is my production of the last four years.

Denied weakness to these medicos (*MM. de Santé*), since she finds new strength for questioning people.

Acting. Dissimulation.

Madame D did her father for six hundred francs, supposedly to pay for a supper which was given this month for her father. *Where did these six hundred francs come from?*

When a person seriously wants to die, they don't seek admission to a clinic like that in the rue Blanche.

Could the doctors not see that the clinic did not involve costs of this kind?

To preserve herself as a married woman (*Se conserver mariée*) !!!

The final humiliation came when Henri Bataille, following well-established literary tradition, based his play *La femme nue* on Debussy's marital affairs, drawing on intimate knowledge of the protagonists. The play was a great success and includes a scene in which Lolette (Lilly) asks Pierre (Debussy) in front of the Princess (Emma) if she (Lolette) must 'return to prostitution'.[16]
Even before these events, Debussy's mood had changed from elation to depression. From Dieppe (where he stayed after Jersey from August to September 1904) he penned these unhappy lines to André Messager: 'I feel nostalgia for the Claude Debussy who worked so enthusiastically on *Pelléas* – between ourselves, I've not found him since, which is one reason for my misery, among others.' After Lilly's suicide attempt, he confesses to his publisher Jacques Durand that he is beginning to be 'hounded' by the press

campaign 'Madame Debussy has been kind enough to launch against me' – all he wants is peace and freedom from 'material complications' (January 1905). Finally, on 7 August 1905, he is able to tell Durand that the nightmare is over – his divorce had come through on 2 August. He has done his duty as a gentleman and is determined 'to live as I want to without bothering about the cheap literature my case will give rise to . . . the facts are really childishly simple'.[17] In fact, Debussy lost the divorce suit, and for the rest of his life, and his heirs' beyond it, litigation from Lilly continued.

Something closer to optimism surfaces in the letters from Eastbourne in 1905. Lilly Debussy had changed her name back to Texier (legally, at any rate), Paris was insufferable – a plague of litigation and scandal – but at least in Eastbourne he had the satisfaction of seeing *La mer* through to publication. Whatever else, his muse had reawakened. The first performance of *La mer* did not build significantly on the success of *Pelléas* at first. This keenly-anticipated event was an anti-climax; but for earlier compositions like *L'après-midi* and *Nocturnes*, '*La mer* washed up these shells and, as it withdrew, it revealed them'.[18] Debussy was now regarded by many as Paris's most important composer.

At the end of the *La mer* period, Debussy acquired limited financial independence after assigning rights of his future works, including *La mer*, exclusively to the publisher Durand in exchange for an annual stipend. Marriage to Emma (20 January 1908) after she divorced her banker husband (1905) should have made Debussy wealthy: she had a rich (and suitably aged) uncle. That he had disinherited her (4 February 1907) meant that Debussy was never to enjoy the material luxury he craved.

It would be foolish to leave the impression that *La mer* is 'about' the breakdown of his marriage. We cannot even say how much of it was composed during or after the breakdown, except for the valuable evidence that the notebook containing the 'journal' includes sketches for the latter part of the second movement and much of the third.[19] It seems reasonable, therefore, to conclude that the troubled waters of the 'Dialogue' reflect the upheaval, while the first movement and much of the second were, in Dietschy's provocative words, 'the premonition of the personal events that would follow . . . Hearing the eternal rumble of the sea as it broke upon the shore, he saw from a distance the purplish waves charging like buffaloes.'[20] Given Debussy's openness to change and the dynamism inspired by the liberating time on Jersey, it may well be that *La mer* became, even during its composition, one of his most personal works, and one of few to deal directly with such deep emotions, channelled through what was for him the most powerful force in nature.

Works

Throughout the known period of *La mer*'s composition (1903–5), Debussy was truly caught between the devil and the deep blue sea. In the month he announced the start of work on *La mer*, he told a friend he was working on his operatic version of Poe's *The Devil in the Belfry*, a project he worked on from 1902 to 1911.[21] Together with an opera based on *The Fall of the House of Usher* (see chapter 4), this should have given the operatic stage a diptych of short operas with strongly contrasted stories. *The Devil in the Belfry* (1835) is the macabre story of a 'rascally little scapegrace' who inflicts chaos on the perfectly running and regimented calm of the Dutch borough of Vondervotteimittiss by making the belfry clock strike thirteen times at noon. One episode and virtually all the libretto were completed (sketches dated August 1903 survive). *La mer* and *The Devil* are related by little more than a thin thread, coincidental perhaps, but one that Debussy cannot have been unaware of: just as *La mer* plays out a natural drama that must have reflected something of the upheaval in his life, so the devil in Poe's story disrupts the routine of Vondervotteimittiss.

Debussy wrote several multi-movement works, most of which lean to the three-movement organisation of *La mer*. The earliest to survive are a movement of a youthful symphony, which exists only in piano-duet form (the manuscript indicates three movements, 'andante', 'air de ballet', 'final', but only an allegro survives), and a piano trio in three movements. Neither work can be accredited with much originality or interest, yet both show how Debussy's style was to develop. One of their most striking features is the lack of clear motivic definition of subject groups. Melodies move primarily by step without making a firm imprint motivically. Rhetorical antecedent–consequent continuations are few and far between, indicating that Debussy had already rejected the strong motivic gestures, with all their denotative import, that he would have heard *ad nauseam* in French and Russian symphonies (see Ex. 1). An effective method of melodic propagation – one that avoided the rhetorical means Debussy mistrusted while still possessing good developmental potential – had still to be found, but his dissatisfaction with the old is not in doubt.

The same problem arises in the undervalued *Fantaisie* for piano and orchestra (1889–90): the opening motif is unmemorable. Here, however, it is compounded by what Vallas and others describe as an excessively heavy adherence to traditional forms. Its most obvious shortcoming for Debussy would have been its close resemblance to d'Indy's *Symphonie sur un chant montagnard français*, especially in the finale; he would have been at his most

Ex. 1   Symphony in B minor, bars 1–5

sensitive in such a matter, not least because it was d'Indy who was proposing to give the première. Debussy withdrew it after rehearsals because d'Indy intended to give the first movement alone, though he may have welcomed this pretext for the other reasons cited. Following this relatively unsuccessful sortie into instrumental forms, Debussy wrote his String Quartet in Franckian cyclic form, achieving a brilliant success within the formal limitations he had set himself. One reason for this is Debussy's discovery of a melodic style that is both distinctive in its intervallic and rhythmic profile, and free from the rhetorical assumptions of his contemporaries. Having found his mature style in an unprecedented freedom of melodic generation, Debussy could now proceed with the string of masterpieces that mark his first maturity. Residual cyclic elements percolate through the multi-movement orchestral works that followed – *Nocturnes*, *La mer*, and *Ibéria*.

For many years it was customary, and acceptable, to perform the first two movements of the *Nocturnes* alone (partly to avoid the expense of a female chorus). David Cox articulates a commonly held view: 'There is no overall unity about the *Nocturnes* . . . because each movement is quite different in style and texture from the others. The same is not true of *La mer* – which is in fact the best symphony ever written by a Frenchman.'[22] A point implicitly reinforced by Debussy when he objected to the dismemberment of *La mer*: '"Jeux de vagues" [second movement] played by itself doesn't seem to me to have the same significance . . . and when you have three children, you can't just take one of them to the Concerts Colonne! . . . The devil take your programme.'[23]

Without claiming that *Nocturnes* is as close to the symphonic ideal as *La mer*, it is arguable that the links between the three *Nocturnes* are stronger than Cox allows. Towards the end of the second of them, 'Fêtes', Debussy's liquidation of the main motivic features brings with it references to both the first and third movements; the relaxation of the fast tempo also draws their expressive characters closer together. Similarly in 'Sirènes', the closing stages produce a synoptic reminiscence of the previous movements in a manner quite distinct from that of *La mer*; yet the effect striven for is unity across the three movements. These convergences of movements run in harness with a cyclic use of a wave-like motif heard at the opening of 'Nuages'. *La mer*'s sense of progression from the first movement to the last, characterised by Howat as a hybrid of sonata form in three movements, is not matched in *Nocturnes*, and in other respects they are characteristic of Debussy's earlier style.[24] The form of all three movements is ternary, with the boundaries blurred in 'Nuages' and 'Sirènes'. The harmonic palette is more conservative, and the polyphonic wealth of *La mer* is barely discernible. Counterpoint takes the form of combining motifs in 'Fêtes' in a manner reminiscent of Berlioz (Debussy engages in a similarly conventional display of contrapuntal technique in the last movement, 'Ballet', of his *Petite suite* for piano duet).

The three orchestral *Images* (1905–12) were first performed separately with the composer's approval, though the three movements of *Ibéria*, the second *Image*, are bound together by motivic recurrences, exchanges of mood, and an *attacca* from 'Les parfums de la nuit' to 'Le matin d'un jour de fête', the last movement. Indeed, a basis of the work is the dissolution of one movement's characteristics into the next. Unlike the movements of *La mer* and *Ibéria*, the three pieces that make up *Estampes* and the first series of *Images* do not seem to make strong claims on each other as a unity; they are, like the orchestral *Images*, collections.

The most substantial achievement of the period of *La mer*, apart from *La mer*, was Debussy's formation of his mature piano style in *Estampes*, *L'isle joyeuse*, *Masques* (1904), and the first series of *Images*. This remarkable series of works reflected Ravel's pioneering piano writing as well as Debussy's own adjustment to the instrument. Here, at last, one finds the compositional outcome of the young Debussy's much-documented experimentation with texture and harmony at the keyboard, which had so outraged and fascinated colleagues and teachers. *L'isle joyeuse* with its ecstatic lyricism and 'symphonic breadth' is the ideal companion piece to *La mer*. Its proportional structure is, on the evidence of Howat's analysis, as carefully wrought as *La mer*'s, and it too makes use of the acoustic scale (see chapter 7). *D'un cahier d'esquisses* (1903) is in Db, the tonic of *La mer*, and makes extensive use of a rhythmic figure that dominates the cello theme of the second principal section (first movement); there is, therefore, a possibility that this piece, about whose genesis little is known, is a spin-off from the composition of *La mer*.

Two song publications, *Trois chansons de France* (1904) and *Fêtes galantes* II (1904), exhibit no obvious connections with *La mer* other than the use of

D♭ major harmony (*La mer*'s final tonic) in the central section of 'Colloque sentimental' (*Fêtes galantes*); significantly, the ghostly lovers address each other in lines like 'Does your heart always beat at the mention of my name'. There is no motivic connection with *La mer*, but the tonal parallel perhaps reinforces the claim that *La mer* encompasses Debussy's 'sentimental storm'.

Danse sacrée et danse profane (1904) is a minor work commissioned by the Maison Pleyel to demonstrate a new chromatic harp without pedals in 1904. The use of continual variation, culminating in cumulative motivic statements, is quite distinct from the style of *La mer*. In contrast, the *Rapsodie* for saxophone and orchestra (1901–11) was, for Debussy, one of the most hateful of commissions; it was begun in 1901 and apparently took up his time in 1903. It was finally sent to the American sponsor Elisa Hall in piano score with some of the bridge passages uncomposed. Its excellent completion and orchestration by Roger Ducasse (1919) reveal one of Debussy's most exotic and at times adventurous conceptions. Oriental sounding arabesque-like melodies make extensive use of modes incorporating intervals of the augmented second, a type wholly excluded from *La mer*. Nevertheless, many have detected an oriental influence upon *La mer* in such passages as the pentatonic melody at I/33, drawing parallels with the sound of gamelan ensembles that made such an impression on Debussy at the Paris Exhibition in 1889. A 1904 commission to provide incidental music for *King Lear* at the Odéon came to nothing. He completed just two orchestral interludes, a fanfare, and 'King Lear's Sleep'. Their main point of interest in a study of *La mer* is that Debussy was working on the project during the period he worked on the end of 'Jeux de vagues' (*La mer*'s second movement) and 'Dialogue du vent et de la mer' (third movement). The most astounding feature of this prolific turnover of works is the diversity of formal, tonal, and motivic procedures followed: even in such a short period, Debussy's abhorrence of self-repetition triumphed.

2

Genesis

Composition

There is no firm evidence that Debussy started writing any part of *La mer* before 1903, but given his long fascination with the sea it is surely possible that something was noted down and stored at an earlier time. This view was shared by Lockspeiser, who, recalling the date of the Mauclair story that originally provided the title of the first movement (1893, around the beginning of composition of *Pelléas*), reflected: 'while we possess no sketches of it from this period it is reasonable to assume that there may have been earlier attempts to give expression to his "endless memories" of the sea.'[1] One such attempt may have been the Franckian principal theme of 'Dialogue du vent et de la mer' (third movement), for although it is perfectly adapted to the music's needs, its character is reminiscent of an earlier phase in Debussy's output.

The visit to René Peter's brother described in chapter 1 is generally thought to have occurred around the time Romain Rolland reported Debussy's engagement on an orchestral work based on *The Fall of the House of Usher*, described as 'a symphony on psychologically-developed themes', in 1890.[2] Keith Spence stumbled upon new information relating to this anecdote in the recollections of a local historian, Dr Petit de la Villéon, writing in 1959, long after the events described (there are no other known sources for this information). Dr Petit moves Debussy's visit to Brittany to 1902–4, the time he 'officially' set to work on *La mer*. After the celebrated sea journey and storm, here taken in the opposite direction, his head was full of themes, but 'as there was no piano in the house he had to try them out on the harmonium in the local church' (the Peter version has Debussy lecturing his friends on programme music from a piano in the Peters' home!). Spence continues:

Could not the 'Iles Sanguinaires' have been, not some Corsican islands that the composer had never seen, but the multitude of rocky islets off the Emerald Coast that glow red in the rays of the setting sun? And what would have appealed more to Debussy's whimsical sense of humour than giving the title 'Dialogue du vent et de la mer' to sea music that had been wheezed out first on an ancient harmonium?[3]

All this may be slightly fanciful; it is certainly at variance with the evidence usually cited and conflicts with Debussy's assertion that he did not function at his best as a composer when in contact with the source of inspiration (see page 13). But Dr Petit's story should not be overlooked.

The first indication that Debussy had started work on *La mer* is a letter dated Friday, August 1903, to Durand from Bichain, the home of his parents-in-law. The casual character of the reference to *La mer* implies Durand's foreknowledge of the project, which is likely, given the many hours Debussy spent in his publisher's company.[4] In spite of this, we can assume that composition cannot have been taken up many weeks prior to the date of the letter, even if some of the ideas had been around much longer (once started, Debussy would have made sure Durand was aware of his activity, for it meant potential advances on royalties). Interestingly, earlier in the same year Debussy mentions the sea in another context; reading between the lines there is no doubt that one of the greatest artistic experiences of the decade for him was the performance of the *Ring* tetralogy in London under the direction of Hans Richter (who had also given the first performance, at Bayreuth). Debussy compares Wagner's music to the sea: 'Among all the hours of boredom . . . the most beautiful things appear. Passages quite beyond criticism and as irresistible as the sea.'[5]

The news of *La mer*'s composition is confirmed on Saturday, 12 September 1903, in a letter to the composer and conductor André Messager in which Debussy denies rumours that he was composing a quintet. In this revealing letter he discloses the original titles of the 'three symphonic sketches'; they were to be '1. "mer belle aux Îles Sanguinaires"; 2. "jeu de vagues"; 3. "le vent fait danser la mer".' He recalls that he had been 'intended for the noble career of a sailor' and had 'retained a sincere devotion to the sea'.

To which you'll reply that the Atlantic doesn't exactly wash the foothills of Burgundy . . . ! And that the result could be one of those hack landscapes done in the studio! But I have innumerable memories, and those, in my view, are worth more than a reality which, charming as it may be, tends to weigh too heavily on the imagination.[6]

So Debussy composed much of *La mer* away from the sea. Except to the most literal-minded people, this hardly seems a matter of great moment: Debussy expressed his passion for the sea on so many occasions that one can be in no doubt that it is a crucial element in the make up of this complex, multi-faceted work. This conversation with Victor Segalen indicates that Debussy was sometimes unable to compose by the sea:

SEGALEN: So you've come from Dieppe!

DEBUSSY: Don't talk about it . . . An absurd visit . . . Can you work by the sea?

SEGALEN: I work more or less anywhere.

DEBUSSY: You're lucky![7]

Debussy often spent his summers at Bichain. It was an ideal rural setting of the kind he invariably sought in the summer months when anxious to replenish and realise his creative energies. On the occasion of the erection of a memorial plaque at the house in the Debussy centenary year (1962), Pasteur Vallery-Radot described the Texier house: 'It was a somewhat dilapidated dwelling, an ancient hostelry. On one side it was bordered by the national road, on the other by a small wood of acacias and poplars, which has now disappeared. He installed a piano there which he rented for 200 francs a year.'[8]

Apart from a loose leaf or two of manuscript lacking musical notation, there are two sets of composition sketches for *La mer* known to us at present. The Sibley manuscript is one of the most fascinating documents associated with Debussy, there being so few sets of sketches for any of his works. It comprises a complete sketch of the work on twenty-eight staved paper, which, following Debussy's usual procedure, is laid out on four staves with a few five-staved exceptions. An exhaustive study of the manuscript was carried out by Rolf; anyone interested in the genesis of *La mer* will wish to read her dissertation, which goes into far more detail than is possible here. Suffice it to say, the sketch is close to the final version of the score, even to the extent of including instrumental details, harmonies, and so on. It was made in black ink over which various annotations appear in different colours (red ink, reddish-brown ink, lead pencil, blue and red pencil). Unfortunately, it was not possible to establish the chronology of the coloured additions due to the rarity of overlapping lines in the different pencils and inks used.[9]

The third movement bears some evidence of haste. Several important motifs are missing, as are accompanying harmonies. In Rolf's opinion this was not so much a reaction to Durand's pressure, which rarely seems to have had much effect, as 'a sureness on his part of content and form in the piece, possibly resulting from the frequent return of motifs and key areas'.[10] One might add that the inspired, unbuttoned character of the movement appears to have made him compose like a man possessed, so potent was the musical and emotional ferment within him.

The other set of sketches, a fairly recent discovery, is much more fragmentary (ms 53).[11] They are a rare example of Debussy's working sketches, located in a notebook recently acquired by the Bibliothèque Nationale; they are for bars 130–1, 163–4, 215–17, and 237–8 of the second movement (bars 219ff, see chapter 6), and several passages from the third, with the notable exception of the principal theme (there are also unidentified sketches). Some of them are clearly intended to amplify or clarify points in the Sibley manuscript, especially points of orchestration and texture – the string parts of III/244, for example – but others surely precede the detail in the Sibley manuscript, indicating that Debussy was not as advanced in the composition of the second and third movements as he had indicated to Durand. Two versions of II/163–4 are shown in Ex. 2. The sketch in ms 53 shows an early stage in the evolution of the accompanying figuration that can be dated with some precision to October 1904 on account of neighbouring entries in the notebook (see also chapter 1); the Sibley manuscript, on the other hand, is almost identical to the final version. This confirms the view that the composition was not completed until the autumn of 1904 at the earliest; orchestration was either taken up immediately afterwards or, more likely, ran concurrently with the composition sketches. Only one sketch, for the end of 'Dialogue du vent et de la mer' (III/278–82), follows the 'journal' in the notebook (this dates from around November or December 1904).

In July 1904 Debussy had fled to Jersey with Emma where he stayed for three weeks before settling in Dieppe for the remainder of the summer. One frequently gets the impression that Debussy was not entirely honest with his publisher, for in September he writes to Durand that he would like to have finished *La mer* in Dieppe, but there was still work to be done on the orchestration, which is as 'tumultuous and varied as the sea itself'.[12] As we have seen, the sketches in ms 53, *pace* Debussy, suggest that there was much composition still to be done. So it is not surprising that in January *and* February 1905 he is entreating Durand's patience for just a 'few more days'.[13]

On Friday, 6 January 1905, Debussy asked his publisher whether he felt 'De l'aube à midi sur la mer' might not be a better title for the first movement than 'Mer belle aux Iles Sanguinaires', giving as his reason 'so many contradictory things dancing around in my head to which this recent flu has added its peculiar dance'.[14] It is not known when he changed the title of the last movement.

One of the last tasks in the composition was the revision of the end of 'Jeux de vagues' so that 'it is neither like a beginning nor an end'; this is mentioned in a letter of 13 January 1905 to Durand.[15] The Sibley manuscript bears the date 'Sunday 5 March 1905 at 6.00 p.m.', and the same date appears at the

Ex. 2a II/163–4 ms 53 (p. 22vo)

Ex. 2b II/163–4 Sibley manuscript (p. 11)

end of the manuscript orchestral score. Since it is inconceivable that the two were finished at the same time, most commentators agree that the sketch was finished beforehand and the date added to the Sibley manuscript at the same time Debussy put the finishing touches to his orchestral score. On the following day he wrote contentedly to the patient Durand, not without some exaggeration, 'My dear friend, relax; *La mer* is finished and has been with the engravers, copyists, etc. since Saturday.'[16]

Above the date on the Sibley manuscript one can just make out an erased dedication: 'pour la p.m. [petite mienne] dont les yeux rient dans l'ombre [whose eyes laugh in the shade]'. This dedication to Emma – arguably so significant for our understanding of *La mer* – was not allowed to stand. Why he replaced it with a straightforward one to his publisher, given the fact he dedicated other works to Emma, is not clear (*Fêtes galantes* II bear the dedication 'In gratitude to the month of June 1904' followed by the letters 'A.l.p.M.' – 'a little mysterious' as Debussy remarked to Durand).[17] The most likely explanation was his discretion and a desire to conceal something with the sort of biographical import Debussy so often kept out of the public gaze; concealment and secrecy are strongly implied by the word 'shade' in the erased dedication.[18]

Second thoughts

L'après-midi was unusual among Debussy's early orchestral works in that it seems to have been presented to the world in a fully finished form that satisfied its composer from the outset. After the first performance it was almost immediately accepted by the public and critics as a key work in the development of French music and needed no subsequent revision. This was not Debussy's usual pattern in orchestral works composed up to *La mer*. The *Nocturnes* were subject to any number of modifications at the composer's behest. Dissatisfaction with the first performance, difficulties encountered in conducting it, the shortcomings of players, and straightforward miscalculations or changes of mind created a maze that makes the production of a definitive score highly problematic. He also made extensive changes to the orchestration of *Pelléas*.

La mer went through a comparable process with the one important difference that many of these changes found their way into the second edition after Debussy had experienced the work from the podium. Nevertheless, the rethinking seems to have been a fluid, continuous process that did not end in 1909, and certainly did not result in a clear-cut expression of Debussy's wishes in the new score. Mistakes still proliferate, and certain features that he seems to have wished to amend remained as they had been in 1905. Broadly speaking, anyone hearing the 1905 score would not notice a great difference. One can say this with impunity for some orchestras retained the original parts for many years (a few still do), and therefore played the first version rather than the second. This is true of Charles Münch's studio recording, which seems to consist entirely of the 1905 edition, and, strange to relate, Pierre Boulez's CBS recording has the 1905 version of I/83 (see page 29).[19]

The most noticeable change of mind is the deletion of the trumpet/horn fanfares in the finale (III/237–44). An unsubstantiated rumour has it that Debussy was told they sounded like part of Puccini's *Manon Lescaut*, an opera by a composer he fervently disliked; so he simply struck them out of the score.[20] In fact there was an intervening stage that can be seen in at least two

Ex. 3   revised version of fanfares (unpublished), III/241–4

copies of the 1905 score with Debussy's hand-written amendments, dating presumably from the years between the editions: he has deleted just the first two fanfares (bars 237–40), leaving the first four notes of the third and all of the fourth (see Ex. 3).[21]

Perhaps Debussy was unhappy with the compositional effect of the fanfares here and was seeking alternative, less drastic solutions before removing them altogether (this evidence tends to contradict the Puccini story – what little of *Manon Lescaut* there was in the fanfares is hardly reduced in the first revision). By the time we get to the 1909 score all trace of them has gone, and Debussy made no attempt to emulate their effect by other means. This change has always been controversial. Rolf laments their excision, arguing that the Puccini reference is barely discernible and that it was a great shame Debussy should have acted so rashly. This was also the view of Ernest Ansermet, who wrote: 'The reason for their suppression . . . remains a mystery. I believe these measures are necessary for the dynamic of this passage and for the contrast with the following episode.'[22] He too had heard of the Puccini story, though he cites a Rome performance as the occasion when the resemblance was pointed out to Debussy, a claim that is not supported by the chronology of the changes. Ansermet, like many conductors, consequently reinstated the fanfares whilst leaving the other 1909 changes intact.[23] Toscanini, who worked from a score apparently amended in consultation with Debussy, left them out, though he made his own modifications elsewhere. Rolf makes the helpful suggestion that the trumpets and horns, instead of playing the fanfares, could double the woodwind and cello line after the manner indicated in the Sibley manuscript.[24] Another change in the finale that is difficult to miss is the revision of the cornet parts in the final bars. Instead of the prominent crotchet triplet figure based on the first cyclic motif (in 1905), they now double the trombones and tuba.

The first movement was also revised, though with a less palpable effect. Two bars were halved in length to produce just one (bar 83), with a striking effect on the proportions of the movement as measured by Howat using the Golden Section (see chapter 6). On a more immediate level, the alteration makes the

Ex. 4   III/110–11, 1905 and 1909 versions

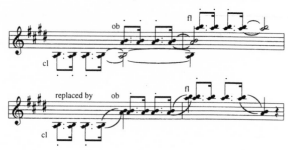

transition to the second principal section less gradual and perhaps counters the tendency for tension to ebb in this transitional passage.

An interesting round of changes involves the alteration of dynamics. These almost always involve the reduction of dynamic levels from, say, *mp* to *p*. No doubt in 1908 orchestras were just as inclined to play too loudly for Debussy's comfort as they are now; his advice to pianists and other performers invariably took the form of exhortations to play more quietly and balance inner voices so that they could emerge clearly. It is remarkable that even in passages where the music is most excitable, he often marks the beginning of a *crescendo* right down to *p*; the penultimate section of 'Jeux de vagues' – II/163–218 – bears abundant evidence of Debussy's use of *piano* markings at even quite an advanced stage in the climactic escalation (most interpreters blithely ignore them). He also adds *en dehors* to many parts that had evidently been submerged in performance, as they often still are in spite of his precautions.

Other changes, especially in the outer movements, mainly involve instrumentation. These are subtle in their effect and generally lean in the direction of lightening the texture, especially at the bass end. As in *Nocturnes*, the highest percentage of changes involves the bassoons and double basses, leading one to wonder if Debussy was motivated by the inadequacies of the players in contemporary orchestras rather than by his own miscalculation; modern recordings that follow the 1905 edition (such as Münch – see chapter 3) indicate that his first thoughts often work perfectly well, even if they sound a trifle richer. Minor accompanying details were also modified, including the woodwind figures in the third movement shown in Ex. 4. The second movement was hardly touched in the revisions.

3

La mer *in performance*

Early performances

Edouard Colonne and Camille Chevillard, directors of the Concerts Colonne and Concerts Lamoureux respectively, were both keen to give the first performance of *La mer*: Debussy's first major work after *Pelléas* was bound to be a highlight of the concert season. After debating the matter, Debussy bestowed the honour upon Chevillard, in spite of his reservations about the first performance of *Nocturnes* at the Lamoureux Concerts in 1900. A letter to Durand (30 September 1903) gives abundant evidence of Colonne's interest in the new Debussy, if not of Debussy's enthusiasm for him: 'The new "Debussy" announced by the gentle Colonne is no less news to me! He has written to me about this, but I still don't know what I will give him; in my plans, *La mer* is destined for Chevillard.'[1] Debussy had been nervous of Colonne ever since the dismal première of the revised *La damoiselle élue* in 1902. It was then that Colonne, aware of his shortcomings or exasperated by the composer's complaints, terrified him by suggesting he conduct the music himself, to which Debussy responded, 'When I have to conduct, I am sick before, during, and after.'[2]

We should pause a moment to consider the first conductor of *La mer*. Chevillard officially took over the Lamoureux Concerts from his father-in-law Charles Lamoureux in 1899, having conducted them for several years. Like most leading French conductors of the period, he was also a composer, with works in traditional forms alongside symphonic poems like *Le chêne et le roseau* (1890). He was a severe figure, nicely evoked by Dominique Sordet, who described

his disenchanted attitude as he mounts the podium, his hostility – more apparent than real – to the public, which manifests itself during those moments that precede the orchestra's first entry. At the least sound in the hall, like a latecomer gliding towards a chair, ill-timed whispering, crumpling of a programme, he turns, stately and outraged, with the ill humour of an old boar discovering a hostile presence in a neighbouring thicket.[3]

In his efficient conducting of the classics, especially Mozart and Beethoven, and fine Wagner interpretations, Chevillard was a key figure in a city that had the richest concert tradition in the world and more concerts, especially on Sundays, than most people knew what to do with. It is interesting to note that Debussy's disenchantment with him, which was exacerbated by the first performance of *La mer*, followed a period of warm and enthusiastic praise in his critical writings. After a performance of Beethoven's Ninth Symphony, Chevillard showed 'an understanding that ranks this conductor among the very greatest', and on another occasion Debussy bore witness to 'an almost unique gift with an orchestra'.[4] Later, Debussy repressed these favourable references when he edited his writings for publication. Now Chevillard 'waves his arms like a news vendor and from behind looks like a bicycle salesman – all of which doesn't exactly make him a thing of beauty'. During the rehearsals for *La mer* Debussy complained of his lack of artistry and suggested he should have been a 'wild beast tamer'.[5]

Debussy's views coincide with others; Chevillard was admirable in the classics, but out of touch with contemporary composers, especially Debussy. In Sordet's view, contemporary music tended to appear in his programmes out of a sense of duty rather than empathy; he 'had little feeling for the latest forms of music – Debussy and his "followers" eluded him. Their impalpable refinements are too delicate for his robust hands.'[6]

With some disquiet Debussy observed a certain dilatoriness on Chevillard's part in the month (March 1905) of *La mer*'s completion, occasioned, it seems, by Chevillard's concern over the work's difficulty – something Debussy felt was being exaggerated. A reluctance to initiate a brawl with Chevillard by contacting Colonne meant that there was little to be done; he left matters for Durand to resolve. Other problems arose when Debussy discovered that Chevillard was considering a performance of *La mer* with music by Wagner in the same programme, sung by the great dramatic soprano Félia Litvinne, at the first concert of the season. He was 'not so arrogant' as to want to be associated in this way with Wagner (Debussy and Wagner were rarely programmed together), and being first in the season, or last, struck him as a dubious distinction, though one he had eventually to put up with.[7]

The oboist M. Fernand Gillet at the première recalled the difficulty of the work and number of rehearsals it necessitated in 1905, painting a picture of conductor and composer at loggerheads. Debussy called out: "*un peu plus vite ici*" . . . So Chevillard said: "*Mon cher ami*, yesterday you gave me the tempo we have just played." Debussy looked at him with intense reflection in his eyes and said: "But I *don't feel the music* the *same way every day*."[8] Proof too that it was high time Debussy took to the rostrum himself so that he could begin to educate orchestral musicians and conductors in the way he coached pianists and singers throughout the latter part of his life.

The programmes for the Concerts Lamoureux that saw *La mer* into the world offer an intriguing glimpse of Paris's musical life at the beginning of the century:

15 October 1905: Beethoven, Symphony No. 7; Franck, Béatitude No. 4; D'Indy, *Symphonie sur un chant montagnard français*; Debussy, *La mer*; Berlioz, *Carnaval romain* overture.

22 October 1905: Lalo, Overture to *Le roi d'Ys*; Haydn, Symphony in D ['London']; Saint-Saëns, *La jeunesse d'Hercule*; Mozart, Aria from *Die Zauberflöte*; Debussy, *La mer*; Franck, Béatitude No. 4; Weber, *Aufforderung zum Tanz* (orch. Weingartner).

At the première, weather conditions were inauspicious for a work that contains one of the most powerful evocations of the midday sun in the entire literature of descriptive music. 'The sky was very overcast . . . fine rain fell incessantly, which should have reminded the critics that drizzle makes the sea dark and sad.'[9] The combination of an unsatisfactory performance, a hostile audience still seething over Debussy's private life, and the novelty of the music militated against a successful outcome. Louis Laloy accounts for the poor showing partly by the fact that the artist had to pay for the sins of the man, and also by enlarging on the view that *La mer* was not what the *Pelléastres* wanted or expected from their idol:

They could no longer rediscover him in the clouds or under the branches of a legendary park, for he had set up his easel on the edge of a sheer cliff where he sought to paint three parts of a composition laid out like a classical symphony with large formal schemes and sustained lines, unfussy and uninhibited – three landscapes evoking the force, the splendour, the joy, and the fear of the sea. It was treason.[10]

La mer had to wait over two years before its real splendour was finally revealed to the public and appreciated by it.

Paris did not get a chance to reassess its largely negative verdict until 1908. There were plans for the Concerts Colonne to play it in 1906, but what Debussy describes as a 'special protocol' prevented this, presumably meaning that Chevillard had come to regard *La mer* as his own property and would retaliate if Colonne played it.[11] Since Chevillard showed himself to be in no hurry for a repeat, it was indeed to be Colonne who undertook to give Parisians their next *La mer*.

On 15 January 1908 Debussy reported to Segalen upon Colonne's decision *not* to conduct *La mer* 'after appalling rehearsals'; instead, the composer himself was to take to the rostrum, as Colonne had been urging him to do (Colonne for his part replaced *La mer* with *L'après-midi* and a suite by Alfred Bruneau entitled *Faute de l'Abbé Mouret*). Debussy had some limited conducting experience with choral societies, but this was the first time he had conducted an orchestral concert, so it was 'not without a furiously beating heart [that] I climbed the rostrum yesterday morning for the first rehearsal'. In spite of his inexperience and fear, Debussy was elated, commenting in the same letter that as a conductor he seemed 'to have become an instrument embracing all possible sonorities, unleashed merely by waving a tiny stick'.[12]

The audience was also well pleased by this concert. It was Debussy's chance to set the record straight after Chevillard's unsatisfactory efforts. Many came to regard this as the real first performance of *La mer*. As well as having in the composer a sympathetic interpreter, the climate in Paris had changed: Debussy's sexual misdemeanours were no longer the main concern – these had been forgotten in the wave of Debussyism now sweeping France. Valery-Radot recalled the great event:

I remember this Sunday where, at three o'clock, at the Châtelet, Debussy appeared from behind the desks of the violins. A sort of frenetic delirium arose from the Debussyists spread around the hall. The ovation ceased only to start again in response to some whistles which Debussy greeted with a gesture of the hand and an ironic smile . . . At the end of the first and second pieces there were explosions of enthusiasm. After the third, bravos and whistles erupted into indescribable mayhem. The ovation continued as Jacques Thibaud started Bach's Chaconne.

He goes on to quote Willy, critic of the *Comœdia*, who wrote that his ears had never heard a fracas comparable to this burst of enthusiasm.[13] In view of the bafflement still expressed by some critics, it is likely that some Debussyists were celebrating their hero rather more than the perceived merits of his music.

Debussy then took *La mer* across the English Channel to London, having incurred some additional financial overheads from his parsimonious publisher on the way: 'Although Debussy was granted a ten per cent reduction on all musical purchases, Durand nonetheless made him pay 4 francs 50 centimes for three conducting batons and buy his own score of *La mer* (15 francs) to send to Henry Wood in January 1908 before his first conducting trip to London!' (Wood thoroughly prepared the orchestra for the performance).[14] Debussy's triumph in London was as momentous as in Paris. Before an ecstatic audience at the Queen's Hall the composer could barely contain himself, sending a telegram to Laloy reporting on the 'Beautiful Sea [the 'Mer belle' of the original title] at the Queen's Hall'.[15] It would be an elaboration to suggest that from this point on Debussy swept all before him on a body-wave of frenzied Debussyists; there was no real echo of Wagnerism or the cult of Bayreuth in the reputation that Debussy was acquiring, but it can be said that 1908 was another watershed in his career, and it was *La mer*, with the reputation of *Pelléas* behind it, that made this year so decisive. However, it was not in Debussy's nature to exploit his new-found popularity: each work was a fresh approach, a refreshment of the tools of his trade, and the audience had to make its way towards him as best it could.

Before Paris had a chance to hear a respectable performance of *La mer* from the composer, on 2 March 1907 Boston (followed by New York) had the inestimable privilege of hearing it under the great Karl Muck, the 'official' *Parsifal* conductor at Bayreuth. Muck rehearsed his fine orchestra, the Boston Symphony, to a level of precision that must have made both Paris performances sound pretty crude. Even those critics who most disliked the work praised the playing, which was 'in the last degree revealing and eloquent' (Lawrence Gilman) and the Boston audience 'heartily applauded' (Philip Hale), even if they, like Gilman, found the work 'elusive . . . it wears none of the hallmarks which long convention has associated with music which assumes to express the sea'.[16]

Gilman had studied the score 'with great diligence', but only when he and other New Yorkers heard it under Toscanini some twenty years later 'were its images and its voices summoned with plenary power from the wraithlike waters of that phantasmal sea'. It was 'a performance that brings the sea about us, swirling through the mind, subduing the senses and the spirit – the sea with its "husky-haughty voice," its timeless fascination, its mystery and its might'. This Debussy concert was sold out: 'when the tumultuous evocation reached its close, with Debussy's tonal sunlight blazing upon a sea of lonely and terrifying splendor, while the music flung its cosmic golden shouts across the haunted void, the house, awed for a moment, burst into a clamorous tumult of applause'.[17]

André Suarès, who had been on the scene for many years and would have had the opportunity to hear the première, shared Gilman's reaction to Toscanini:

I found the greatest triumph of Toscanini, of his intelligence and his art, in his performance of *La mer*. Perhaps he alone has made me feel the extraordinary power of this work. It isn't the thunder and lightning nor the orchestral cataclysm that bring grandeur and force to this symphony. I see in it the greatest and most beautiful musical poem in French music.[18]

Post 1918: Paris

Paris remained a city of extraordinary musical activity after the war, enjoying a variety of concerts unmatched in the Paris of the 1990s (New York or London might be more suitable comparisons). The winter season of 1920 was typical. On Sunday, 23 October, audiences could hear Rhené-Baton conducting the first two *Nocturnes* at the Concerts Pasdeloup at 3.00 p.m., and they might then run down to the Théâtre Châtelet to hear Gabriel Pierné conduct *Ibéria*. Four days later we find *L'après-midi* at the Concerts Touche, and again on 1 November and 4 November (Concerts Rouge), and then finally *La mer* at the Concerts Lamoureux under the work's first conductor, Chevillard, on 7 November. More performances of the *L'après-midi* followed at various concert venues on 18, 21, 27, and 28 November, 12, 16, 17, 18, and 24 December! Apparently Paris's appetite for this work was insatiable: within a couple of weeks of the new year it featured in several more programmes. *La mer* was also heard again in 1920, at the Concerts Pasdeloup on 18 December. Even this ratio of *La mer* performances to those of *L'après-midi* is perhaps too biased in favour of *La mer* to be fully representative; in the following years *La mer* might only be heard once or twice whereas the *L'après-midi* would be on the menu at least once, if not twice, a week. Other works that cropped up fairly often – more than *La mer* – are the String Quartet (often represented by its slow movement only), the first two *Nocturnes*, and Lia's air from *L'enfant prodigue*.[19]

The programmes continue to look mouth-watering. On 31 May 1921, the Orchestre Colonne under Pierre Monteux, once a viola player in the orchestra, played three Wesendonck-Lieder, three *Songs and Dances of Death* (Musorgsky), Griffes' *Pleasure Dome*, *Sheherazade*, and *La mer*. Les Concerts Staram started in January 1926 with an enterprising repertoire that fully recognised Debussy's leading position among modern French composers. In their first season of ten concerts all three orchestral *Images* and *La mer* were performed. Walther Staram's interpretations were, apparently, of the highest quality. By this stage, however, programming *La mer* was hardly a radical departure for a concert promoter.

Critical opinion

Critical reaction to the première was variable. Alongside a few torrents of abuse such as any progressive new work might expect from entrenched critical opinion, there were various degrees of perplexity, hostility, and, in a few quarters, enthusiasm. Apart from Debussy's marital misconduct, many who were keen on *Pelléas et Mélisande* were upset by the marked change in the composer's style. Where the sea had been remote and muted in the opera, it now sounded strident and forward. Debussy had moved on.

An intriguing review came from a critic who had, after some persuasion, been a staunch supporter of *Pelléas*. Pierre Lalo failed to hear the sea:

Think of the grotto scene in *Pelléas*: a few chords and a single orchestral rhythm give you the entire atmosphere of night and of the sea . . . It seems to me that in *La mer*, the sensibility is neither so intense nor so spontaneous; I think that Debussy desired to feel, rather than actually felt, a deep and natural emotion. For the first time in listening to a descriptive work of Debussy's I have the impression of beholding not nature, but a reproduction of nature, marvellously subtle, ingenious and skilful, no doubt, but a reproduction for all that . . . I neither hear, nor see, nor feel the sea.[20]

Debussy's unusually prickly reaction to this 'unkindest cut' inspired one of his most celebrated letters: 'I love the sea and I've listened to it with the passionate respect it deserves. If I've been inaccurate in taking down what it dictated to me, that is no concern of yours or mine. You must admit, not all ears hear in the same way.' Lalo also criticised Debussy's music for lacking logic and being held together by (in Debussy's words) 'a tenacious sensibility and a dedicated search for the "picturesque"', so eliciting this comment: 'The heart of the matter is that you love and defend traditions which, for me, no longer exist or, at least, exist only as representative of an epoch in which they were not all as fine and valuable as people make out; the dust of the past is not always respectable.'[21]

These two accusations, lack of logic or formlessness on one hand, too little evidence of the sea on the other, run through much criticism of *La mer*. However, there were also some quite astute reactions, including that of Gaston Carraud, who was one of few outside Debussy's inner circle (Laloy, quoted above, was a close friend and ally of Debussy's) to recognise a new strength of formal purpose; he also offered his readers an insight into the new direction taken on the programmatic side:

The three symphonic pieces . . . do not give any complete idea of the sea, they depict only a few of its aspects as seen at close quarters. Nor do they express the essential characteristics of the sea, but rather those ever-delightful frolics in which she exhausts her divine energy, and the lively interplay of water and light that so bewitches us: the magic spell of foam and wave and spray, swirling mists and splashes of sunlight. Nor is the term 'sketches' well adapted to these pieces, for their structure, though slight, is logical and strong, as in all Debussy's compositions; in fact it is clearer and more definite than in his previous works.

He goes on, however, to charge Debussy with being more derivative in *La mer* than in his other orchestral works, finding traces of the Russians and Franck. His final comment had no appeal to Debussy: in detecting greater brilliance and less mystery, he utters the grim prophecy that one day they might find themselves with an 'americanized Debussy'.[22]

Gilman excepted, Debussy's reception in Boston and New York was largely negative. Among the barbs hurled at him were 'meaningless rubbish of the dreariest sort' and 'more of barnyard cackle than of the moods and voices of the sea'.[23] Nevertheless, the quality of some of the more sympathetic writing would be hard to match in modern English or American criticism, such as this evocative piece by the Harvard-educated Henry Taylor Parker (always known as 'H.T.P.'):

The tale used to go that Debussy had sat in barracks on the outskirts of Paris and watched clouds hour upon hour. He may have watched the sea as endlessly. But the clouds of the Nocturne and the sea of the orchestral sketches are also and equally the clouds and the sea of a poet's vision. They are not the things themselves, like the delineations of Strauss's music. They are Debussy's dream of them, and the secrets that they tell him . . . [there is] little sense of melodies, of rhythms, of figures in the ordinary sense of the words, and none of the relations of music that custom has made arbitrary.[24]

After the 1908 performance in Paris, we find a thoughtful but still unsympathetic treatment by Jean Chantovoine in the influential *Courrier musical*:

Choosing his themes and harmonies, and excluding rhythm, so that they are as lifeless as dried plants in a herbarium, M. Debussy next distributes his material, lays it out, and fits it as best he can into four, eight, or sixteen bars, which four, eight, or sixteen other bars will presently reproduce more or less exactly.[25]

Controversy continued to surround *La mer* and its author until war curtailed it. As performances improved in quality and quantity, however, the shocking novelty of its musical structures lost its capacity to baffle, just as Debussy's rebuttal of the rhetorical means of evoking the sea ceased to alienate.

Performance styles

An 'authentic' *La mer* is an unthinkable, unobtainable concept, especially if by 'authentic' we mean an attempt to recreate the first performances as closely as possible. For one thing, these performances were unsatisfactory interpretatively; they seem to have made little impression on most of the audience, and the composer himself was unimpressed. When Debussy took up the cause of *La mer* in 1908, it may well be that the spirit of the work began to emerge from the still unfamiliar notation (reports on his conducting are mixed), but he was an inexperienced conductor, unable, one imagines, to do more than give a creditable play-through of the work. When he conducted the Queen's Hall Orchestra a few days later, Henry Wood had already rehearsed the score with the players, presumably influencing the eventual performance. If, as Norman Lebrecht maintains, a virtuoso conductor could be a vital part in the success of a work, for example, 'Nikisch founded Tchaikovsky's popularity in Germany [and elsewhere]', then the work of conductors like Koussevitzky and Toscanini, who were trusted and admired by Debussy, must be crucial links in the formation of a performing style for *La mer*. The decline of the virtuoso conductor in recent years and the improved technical facility of orchestral players will also have an impact on the way *La mer* is heard today.[26]

If we take two vital pieces of evidence as source material for a discussion of an 'authentic' *La mer* – the score and the sound of French orchestras in Debussy's time – it becomes clear that most conductors have departed radically from Debussy's intentions. There is no reason why we should assume that Debussy wanted *La mer* to be played exclusively by French orchestras, even though his main musical experiences would have been of the Concerts Colonne, Lamoureux, and others, but the score points to a style of woodwind playing, for example, that is difficult for a modern orchestra but ideally suited to the distinctive capabilities of French orchestras of the pre-war years. The rapidly-repeated chords for flute and clarinets in the second movement, first heard in bar 60, not only require very rapid articulation, but two varieties of inflection have to be observed, namely a tenuto over the quaver, and staccato over the triplet semiquavers, all to be played *piano* and *très léger* (see Ex. 5). Modern performances, even the select few that approach Debussy's metronome marking of crotchet = 138, rarely achieve the lightness and fleet dexterity apparently required. In case one feels the score is over-demanding, one need only turn to Piero Coppola's fascinating 1932 set with the venerable L'Orchestre de la Société des Concerts du Conservatoire to discover its closest imaginable realisation, with attendant advantages for the audibility of the *piano* harp figures marked *decrescendo* and the sustained chord in the horns and cellos.[27] Without full observance of the woodwind notation, balance becomes awkward; from what we know of Debussy's views on performance, dynamics and balance were paramount.

Other timbral attributes of French orchestras before 1939 also favoured an

Ex. 5   II/60–1

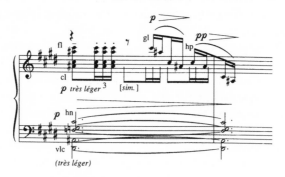

accurate realisation of *La mer*'s textural complexities. In Coppola's recording, the violins, for instance, though largely lacking the portamento of the same orchestra in 1918 or even 1928 (on recorded evidence), had a lean, crisp sonority with a refined, sometimes negligible amount of vibrato. The effect is comparable to the use of gut strings in that it thins out the sound, enabling woodwind and harps to emerge more clearly in intricate passages such as II/62ff. With such playing, details emerge without the need to force them through, and because the players are playing at a moderate dynamic, the varied articulation Debussy demands is possible; the orchestral sound is wonderfully variegated as a result.

This was only the second recording; the first was also by Coppola with an *ad hoc* orchestra and inferior sound (1928).[28] In 1935, a live recording of the greatest interest was made by BBC engineers in London's Queen's Hall with Toscanini and the BBC Symphony Orchestra. The different style of playing is striking, including thicker woodwind sound, more string vibrato, and less flexibility in rapid passages. The personalities of the two conductors must also be responsible for the changing presentation of *La mer*. Toscanini, reared in the Italian tradition of melody with accompaniment, enriched by a thorough immersion in the Austro-German classics culminating in the works of Wagner, Brahms, and Strauss, had less empathy for the different construction of Debussy's music with its subtle layering of sound that, to some extent, invalidated the familiar *Hauptstimme–Nebenstimme* opposition.[29] Following the Straussian manner, voices are pushed to the fore, creating an artificial hierarchy of melody and accompaniment; the dynamics of the horn melody from I/35 are exaggerated, *piano* markings are stepped up in volume, and greater effort is spent on producing the saturated sound of the Wagnerian tutti, not least in the climax at III/195 whose Romantic character is exaggerated by Toscanini and, many years later, by Karajan, both of whom amplify the *forte* marking in the strings and ignore or underplay the *diminuendo* in the accompaniment.

Toscanini's brightly-lit performances had a cathartic effect on contemporary audiences, but it is debatable whether they represented the final, definitive revelation of *La mer* or just a very impressive exhibition of the virtuoso conductor's art. One decidedly negative aspect of Toscanini's *La mer* was his modification of passages, including two pages of full score that 'he actually rewrote . . . and pasted . . . into his copy in place of the authentic text'.[30] Under Toscanini's direction, as under Koussevitzky's, *La mer* became an orchestral showpiece of the first order – a noisier, more brilliant work than seems justified by the authority of the score or the illuminating Paris recordings.

Few conductors since have thought it worthwhile to question many of the assumptions that have been made about *La mer*. The resultant distortions are only partly charted in Table 1, which compares ten historically or interpretatively interesting performances (no attempt is made to quantify fidelity to dynamic markings, balance, and other potentially subjective categories).

1. The three most significant differences between the 1905 and 1909 editions are the compression of two bars into one (I/83), the deletion of four horn/ trumpet fanfares (III/237ff), and the replacement of the cornets' high crotchet triplets (III/286–9 – see chapter 2). Only performances that follow 1905 throughout would be expected to reinstate the two bars in the first movement, so Boulez's lapse from 1909 in the first movement is inexplicable, unless sloppy tape editing is to blame. Conductors who otherwise follow the 1909 score often reinstate the fanfares in the finale; whereas many early conductors, including Toscanini and Coppola, omitted them, this has now become standard practice. Szell's recording is curious: he follows 1909 in deleting the fanfares, but retains the high cornet parts in the closing pages, producing a strange mixture that suggests he was following the 1938 edition (a recent recording by Yan Pascal Tortelier also has the 1905 cornet parts).

2. Debussy specifies a crotchet pulse of 116 at the opening of 'De l'aube à midi sur la mer', which may seem fast for *Très lent*, but the underlying rhythmic unit is the minim, so the effect would still be of a slow tempo. This tempo should be applied to the quaver of the following *modéré* (I/31), presumably with the acceleration prior to it (bars 23ff) converting crotchets at 116 to quavers at 116. Debussy's metronome markings are explicit: he wanted the connection, but only one or two conductors attempt it. The remainder often begin at around crotchet = 80 in the introduction and

Table 1 A comparison of recorded performances of *La mer*

	Monnard	Coppola 1932	Toscanini 1935	Münch 1956	Szell 1960	Inghelbrecht 1962	Karajan 1964	Ansermet 1964	Boulez c. 1968	Ashkenazy 1986	Solti 1991
1. 1905/1909 version											
bar I/83		1909	1909	1905	1909	1909	1909	1909	1905!	1909	1909
III/237ff fanfares					1909	1909	1905	1905	1909	1905	1905
III/286ff cornets					1905		1909	1909	1909	1909	1909
2. Opening tempos											
I/1 Très lent ♩ = 116	♩ =	88	104	80	80	76	104	96	76<80	92>72	104
I/31 Modéré sans lenteur ♪ = 116	♪ =	104<116	120>104	116>96	116>100	126>104	108<116	116<138	116<120	116<120	116>108
3. I/84–end	*Monnard*										
I/84 Un peu plus mouvementé	*♩ = 69*	52	52	52	63	48	42	54	54	54	44
I/86 Très rythmé	*♩ = 104*	52<76	76	72	76	66<88	69	54<88	76	76<92	76
I/98 au Mouvt (un peu plus m'menté)	*♩ = 69*	96	88<92	100	76	92	88	72<88	88<92	84	80
I/109 En retenant peu à peu		92	72	76	63	58	72	58	88	80	66
I/112 Encore plus retenu	*♩ = 58*	76	58	63	54	54	69	60	80	69	63
I/119 Presque lent		63	44	54	48	44	52	50	63	48	56
I/122 Très modéré ♩ = 104		76	80	69	84	86	80	96	88	69	92
I/132 Très lent ♪ = 80		72	96<100	63<80	76	72	63<69	50<84	66	52<72	58<76
4. Principal theme III/56–118	*𝅗𝅥 =*										
III/56–71 Cédez très légèrement et	*bar 56*	72	69	66	80	72	69	76	76	80	63
retrouvez peu à peu le mouvement initial	*bar 60*	80	72	72	96	84	88	88	84	92	76
[from 𝅗𝅥 = 96 at III/1]	*bar 65*	76	76	72	80	80	72	76	80	88	80
III/72 Tempo I° [𝅗𝅥 = 96]	*bar 72*	80	92	84	88	76	84	88	84	88	84<88
	bar 94	92	96	88	92	76	84	80	96	92	88<92
	bar 115	108	100	96	88	80	84	84	100	96	92

accelerate to 116 in the first principal section. Karajan's tempos are the most closely related of those sampled – Boulez and Inghelbrecht's least so.

3. I/84–98. The tempo markings here may seem unambiguous, yet no performance known to me follows them. Jean-François Monnard, whose article on faults in the performance of *La mer* is invaluable, writes of the opening of the second principal section:

> The *Très rythmé* . . . that applies to the cellos' phrase is never respected because the indication is missing from the orchestral parts, and the players cannot comprehend the intentions of a conductor with the disagreeable idea of rushing them.[31]

Another problem arises in bar 98 where Debussy indicates *au Mouvt (Un peu plus mouvementé)*. Presumably the brackets are for clarification, signalling that the tempo to be returned to is that of I/84, where *Un peu plus mouvementé* occurs, so crotchet = 69 (Monnard's view). In view of the music's character in bar 98, it may be argued that *au Mouvt* refers to bar 86 instead, but Debussy's bracketed clarification seems to deny this, as do the demi-semiquavers in bars 100ff, which often cause conductors to slow down suddenly or risk smudging the notes. Whichever interpretation is correct, a reduction in pulse is surely intended at bar 98, so it is perplexing that neither reading finds favour with the sampled performances: all but Szell and Ansermet add to the already animated tempo and are then forced to make drastic reductions to meet the *rit.* to *Presque lent* in bar 119.

4. The principal theme of 'Dialogue du vent et de la mer' should begin with a *Cédez* followed by an acceleration back to Tempo 1, to be completed at bar 72 when the second limb of the theme takes over. Performances rarely observe this marking (a last-minute addition to the score absent from both the orchestral manuscript and piano–duet version) precisely: of those sampled, Toscanini, Münch, and Solti come closest to Debussy's intentions. Deviations from the score vary: the majority of conductors make a substantial *rit.* in bar 63 and begin the gradual *accel.* afresh in bar 65, a few simply ignore the instruction altogether (not those sampled), and most carry the *accel.* beyond the Tempo primo of bar 72, often making a striking increase in speed at the start of, or during, the ostinato of bars 94ff. Coppola and Toscanini are extreme in the range of tempos used: both increase the pulse by around fifty percent between bars 56 and 118. Szell, characteristically, limits tempo changes, though he too makes a substantial *rit.* at bar 63.

31

4

The 'invisible *sentiments of nature*'

Musical seas

Composers have written music in celebration of the sea and other watery phenomena for centuries. In one very beautiful example, Mozart evokes the gentle wind and calm waves in the Act I trio from *Così fan tutte*, 'Soave sia il vento'. Here the wind and sea are entwined together in a union that is rarely broken in later sea music. Muted strings play an undulating figure of a sort that was to feature prominently in the impressionist parts of Wagner and the 'real' Impressionists who followed.

The sea is often not the main subject; rather, it provides the context for human actions, or acts as a metaphor for human emotions. A rare exception is Mendelssohn's exquisite *Hebrides* overture, which seems to place the changing character of the sea at the heart of the composition. Debussy had a low opinion of Mendelssohn in general, describing him as an 'elegant and facile notary',[1] but it is difficult to imagine so popular a water piece failing to make some impression on him.

The sea is an important element in Wagner's operas, as are the River Rhine and other inland waters, but perhaps the most important work in the evolution of French musical Impressionism (however little one may like the term, it is invariably used in historical writing to characterise this period and works by Chabrier, Debussy, Dukas, and others) was a short orchestral piece that is not much concerned with water at all. *Forest Murmurs* is a clever arrangement of the lyrical episodes that precede and follow the young Siegfried's murderous activities in Act II of *Siegfried*. In spite of its subject-matter being the murmurs of the forest and bird-song, the musical iconography of pairs of undulating pitches, which had been used by Mozart, was still being appropriated to depict the movement of water (Wagner had already used them to accompany the appearance of the Rhinegold motif in Scene 1 of *Das Rheingold*). Debussy made little use of conventional water motifs or figures in *La mer*, yet he still finds a place for this genus at the beginning of the first principal section of 'De l'aube à midi sur la mer' (bar 31).[2]

The 'bleeding' chunks drawn from Wagner's operas, such as the *Forest Murmurs* and *Magic Fire Music*, so vital to the propagation of his music in France (where the operas waited many years for their first performances), constitute a genre in their own right, one that offers a fascinating precedent for the forms and style of Debussy, as for many of his contemporaries. The overture to *Der fliegende Holländer* is a fine example of the combination of sea imagery, storm, and the kind of narrative that was so often set against its backdrop. Here is a typical operatic sea drama in which the anger of the sea acts as an allegory for the turbulent destiny of the anti-hero. As in many such dramas, the feminine character is depicted in gentle woodwind tones with the archetypal Romantic motif of the descending third. However remote, the principal theme of 'Dialogue du vent et de la mer' also has a 'feminine' character (in a specific Romantic sense) that is set against the stormy music of the sections that precede and follow it.[3]

The search for *La mer*'s musical antecedents reaches an interesting juncture when account is taken of symphonic works entitled *La mer* by Victorin de Joncières and Paul Gilson. Unlike Glazunov's fantasy *Morye* (The Sea, 1889), whose musical substance and programme are inspired by Liszt's tone poems, these *La mer*s are products of the French musical renaissance of which Debussy was a very superior part. De Joncières' evocation of the sea, *La mer*, is in four movements, namely 'The calm', 'Contemplation', 'The tempest', and 'Epilogue', which set poetry by E. Guinaud for soprano (as the 'voice of the sea') and chorus. Its relative conservatism is evidenced by its première at the staid Conservatoire Concerts on 9 January 1881. Massenet-like feminine cadences rub shoulders with a rich harmonic language shot through with Franckian chromaticism and resourceful orchestral effects. There are cyclic elements. In the third movement, 'The tempest', the extent of Debussy's originality becomes ever clearer as one encounters the clichés de Joncières had recourse to in his musical portraiture: tremolos and rocking figures of foreboding, lightning streaks in the flute and piccolo, a rumbling chromatic bass line, and so on. Nevertheless, the passage quoted in Ex. 6, from the opening of this movement, is not totally unlike the opening of Debussy's third movement; it at least demonstrates the extent to which residual nineteenth-century programmatic elements lingered on in Debussy's own, far more subtle musical iconography.

Gilson's *La mer* (1892) is an ambitious orchestral work prefaced in the score with poems by Eddy Levis, and composed on the cyclic principle. At the end of the Finale, the cyclic motif in its original, first-movement form is restated with an almost Brucknerian emphasis. This motif is typical of cyclic motifs

Ex. 6   Victorin de Joncières, *La mer*, bars 4–7

of the time, as is shown by the opening of Debussy's contemporary *Fantaisie* for piano and orchestra (see chapter 2), which also hovers around the sixth note of the major scale (see Exx. 7 and 8). The four movements are titled – 'Sunrise', 'Sailors' Songs and Dances', 'Twilight', 'Tempest' – and one can only admire the adventurous orchestration which includes multiple division of the strings and light, rapid pitch repetition marked staccato in the

Ex. 7   Paul Gilson, *La mer*, bars 4–12

Ex. 8   Debussy, *Fantaisie* for piano and orchestra, bars 1–4

Ex. 9   Gilson, *La mer*, 'Twilight', cue 39+9

woodwind which adumbrates 'Jeux de vagues' (see Ex. 5). In the third movement ('Twilight') other features look tentatively forward to Debussy: the harmony is initially ambiguous and chromatic, and there are *lontano* effects involving distant horns; arabesque-like figures are also found, especially in the woodwind (see Ex. 9). The style is, in most other respects, related to Liszt and Franck; like the de Joncières *La mer*, the harmonic resources are progressive in the Franck-d'Indy manner, so no matter how chromatic and far-reaching the activity in between, the main cadences are based on orthodox I–V–I progressions. Even so, it is surely no coincidence that Debussy adopted Gilson's subtitle, 'symphonic sketches'. When Debussy's *La mer* was first heard in Brussels, an enterprising concert promoter had the bright idea of programming the two *La mer*s on successive evenings. On this occasion it was Gilson whose work was well known and popular; Debussy's was the newcomer.[4]

Impressionism

The sea conjured up in Debussy's *La mer* has proved so fascinating that no effort has been spared to identify it with the work of other artists and schools. This has often taken the form of a debate concerning the merits of the title 'Impressionist composer' that so many have bestowed upon Debussy. It is a fractious subject, for some, such as Roger Nichols in his *New Grove* entry on Debussy, would much prefer to identify him with the Symbolist movement, while a solid remainder opts to leave Debussy unclassified.[5] Lockspeiser, one of Debussy's finest scholars, was unequivocal: '*La mer* is the greatest example of an orchestral Impressionist work', he declares as he sums up his discussion of the 'network of associations . . . which prompted the composition of *La mer*'.[6]

Impressionist painters rendered the atmosphere or sensation around external things, illustrating the 'truth' behind them in preference to their geometric form. In music the term 'Impressionism' is on loan, with all the dangers that entails. So far as we can tell, *La mer* is not an attempt to paint the sea as it was filtered through the musician's imagination or play of light. Debussy 'freed music from the semantic approach', leaving no external object to be filtered.[7] What Debussy recorded of his creative process, as much as our own response to the music, suggests that *La mer* is devalued by interpreting it as representation.

Impressionism in painting has as much to do with technical means as aesthetic objectives. The way colour is distributed on the canvas, the new treatment of perspective, and the loosening of other classical techniques were crucial in the evolution of modern painting. Whatever attitude we have to the description of Debussy's artistic goals as Impressionistic, one has to be wary of extending the term to his musical technique. Lockspeiser in his inadequate discussion of Debussy's musical language resolutely refuses to define Debussy's tonal procedures, preferring instead to quote the Belgian composer Gilson, whose own *La mer* preceded Debussy's by fifteen years: 'This is ornamental music in the broadest sense of the term . . . The instrumental works in question appear to consist of a series of impressions connected by "repeats" and their instrumentation is accordingly the same as Debussy's harmony itself, entirely impressionistic.'[8] By impressionistic harmony he means non-functional – a chord or series of chords thought up for the pleasure of the moment, for the fleeting impression granted the listener. 'Non-functional' implies harmony that has turned its back on the old series of hierarchically-arranged dominants and tonics, and the carefully ordered resolution of dissonance, in favour of a succession of harmonic colours for their own sake. It is seen as a musical analogue to the loosening of representation in Monet's paintings, to which the response is that *La mer* is highly organised tonally, only not according to the principles of the nineteenth century. It is unarguable that Debussy followed his whim in matters harmonic, as well as formal, making his pleasure the arbiter rather than the 'rule books' still partly adhered to by his contemporaries.[9] But this does not make his music less logical or well structured; it merely ensures that the language is different. To write off the technical procedures of a finely crafted work like *La mer* with words like 'ornamental', no matter how broadly connoted, is damaging, for it denies *La mer* an intellectual rigour in its use of tonality, form, and so on. It is preferable to allow that Debussy's language is new, which is undeniable, and then be broadminded about his artistic intentions. As Arnold Whittall says: 'Debussy himself ultimately felt closer to Mallarmé than to Monet, and in calling him . . . an impressionist we are ourselves producing a blurred, ambiguous image.'[10]

Whether Debussy belongs to the Impressionists or not, he and Monet are related by similarities of experience. Seascapes are among Monet's most famous paintings. John House describes Monet's objectives in some of the great canvases that date from the last decades of the nineteenth century: 'Once he was fully accustomed to a place, Monet tended to emphasise either elemental forces or atmospheric effects.' In his travels in the 1880s, he 'often chose subjects which showed nature at its most elemental, particularly emphasising the opposing forces of land and sea'. Belle-Isle attracted him greatly: 'For three days now we've had a dreadful storm; I've never seen such a spectacle . . . I'm trying to do some quick sketches of this upheaval, because it's marvellous'. There are anticipations of Debussy's sea experiences here. A few days later Monet described the strength of his feelings for the sea: 'You know my passion for the sea, and it is so beautiful here . . . I feel that every day I'm understanding it better . . . its effect is quite terrifying . . . I'm mad about it'.[11] Among his paintings, works like *Storm, Coast of Belle-Isle* (1886)[12] must be accounted forerunners of 'Dialogue du vent et de la mer'.

Turner's seascapes were admired by Debussy, who described Turner as the 'finest creator of mystery in the whole of art!'[13] The dramatic use of space and light in Turner's paintings must surely have been a more potent element in the make-up of Debussy's response to the sea than the celebrated print by the Japanese artist Katsushika Hokusai, 'The hollow of the wave off Kanagawa' (from *Thirty-six Views of Mount Fuji*, c. 1820–9), chosen by Debussy for the front cover of *La mer* (1905 edition of the orchestral score). Hokusai's influence was admittedly considerable in France during the evolution of Impressionist and Post-Impressionist painting (Monet possessed copies), and his appeal to Debussy was such that the composer kept the print on the wall of his office. The original shows, in a highly stylised form, three 'boats, manned by desperate crews . . . almost submerged in what appears to be a terrifying storm'. The version reproduced by Durand leaves only a crudely simplified version of the wave. Nonetheless, this was clearly an appropriate cover for *La mer* in view of the tempest that erupts in 'Dialogue du vent et de la mer'. Even if *La mer* in some way alludes to the print, it takes a leap of faith to accept Lockspeiser's view that a 'contributing factor [to *La mer*'s] firmer strength of design . . . may well have been the assimilation within the Impressionist vision of the aesthetic of Hokusai and Hiroshige'.[14]

Programme

Debussy's attitude to programmatic music is well documented. In a review of a performance of Beethoven's *Pastoral* Symphony he wrote:

certain of the old master's pages do contain expression more profound than the beauty of a landscape. Why? Simply because there is no attempt at direct imitation, but rather at capturing the *invisible* sentiments of nature. Does one render the mystery of the forest by recording the height of the trees? It is more a process where the limitless depths of the forest give free rein to the imagination.[15]

These views are reinforced in an interview he gave to Emily Frances Bauer:

I live in a world of imagination, which is set in motion by something suggested by my intimate surroundings rather than by outside influences, which distract me and give me nothing. I find an exquisite joy when I search deeply in the recesses of myself and if anything original is to come from me, it can only come that way.[16]

Although much of Debussy's output is programmatic to the extent that individual movements carry descriptive titles, his comments about Beethoven precisely define the limitations he placed upon pictorialism or Impressionism in music. Debussy's music was not usually concerned with describing anything as specific as Strauss's arrival at an Alpine summit or d'Indy's boisterous peasants disporting themselves in the valley, but rather with a remarkable synthesis of the natural world and human emotion, harnessed together in such a way as to become indivisible. Jarocinski elaborates this point in his discussion of *Pelléas*: 'What interested him much more than the mere experiencing of phenomena was to associate them with thoughts and feelings ... the theme in arabesque at the beginning of the second act does not imitate the sound of the fountain in the garden ... it suggests fluidity in general.'[17] The same surely applies to the arabesques at the opening of 'Jeux de vagues'.

The discarded title of the first movement, 'Mer belle aux Iles Sanguinaires', is from a short story by Camille Mauclair, an important commentator on the Impressionist movement. It has now been appended to an article in which Rolf considers its possible contribution to the first movement. The story 'depicts a fateful voyage at sea in a boat headed for three of the Sanguinary Islands. The explorers stop at each island, which represent [*sic*] in an allegorical way the passage of time, and eventually are left disillusioned and stranded on the final island, never to return.' Rolf discovers a parallel between the story's three stages and the subdivisions of the first movement of *La mer*, which are marked by restatements of the first cyclic motif. Also, both story and symphonic movement 'display a quality of gradual progression or continuous transformation from their beginnings to their ends'. There may be a convergence between a specific literary source and part of *La mer* here, though the evidence is not strong (the general tenor of the story seems far removed from the first movement); it may also be nothing more than Debussy taking a fancy to a nice-sounding title.[18] In any case, he dropped it in favour of one that conveys a 'gradual progression' explicitly. Rolf speculates on another literary source, Pierre Louÿs's *Sanguines*, which Debussy was reading in 1903. The short story 'Escale en rade de Nemours' includes 'a vivid description of a storm at sea'.[19]

In the questionnaire mentioned in chapter 1, Debussy names but one favourite poet, Baudelaire, whose celebrated sea poems must have been well known to him and helped shape his response to it. Baudelaire's oceans find an echo in Jules Michelet's popular *La mer* (published 1861), a brilliant philosophical and speculatively scientific work. In chapter 6 the author describes the three forms of nature 'attending and enlarging our soul':

The variable ocean of the air, with its festival of light, its vapours and chiaroscuro, its mobile phantasm of capricious creations, so rapidly evaporating.

The fixed ocean of the earth, its undulation that one follows astride great mountains, the upheavals that testify to its ancient movement, the sublimity of the summits, perpetually frozen.

Finally the ocean of the waters, less mobile than the first, and less fixed than the second, responsive to celestial movements in its regular equilibrium.

The greatest difference between the three was that the 'ocean speaks':

The ocean is a voice. It speaks to distant galaxies, responds to their movements in its grave and solemn language. It speaks to the earth, to the shore, with a moving tone, in harmony with their echoes; plaintive, menacing by turns, it growls or sighs. It speaks to humanity above all . . . All of that combined and blended is the great voice of the ocean.

Perhaps Debussy would have found fault with the way Michelet places humankind at the centre of all things, but his sea is surely akin to Debussy's. Laloy, among others, detected the call of the sea in the 'symphonic sketches', and Charles Malherbe, who wrote the programme notes for the 1908 performances presumably from information given to him by Debussy, used terms reminiscent of Michelet: 'before this great spectacle of the sea [at Jersey], by turns caressing and furious, the symbol of life, in this splendour of waves that surge and of winds that roar, the composer has endeavoured to take down the voice of the ocean'. Some refer to the first cyclic motif as the 'call of the sea' or a 'melancholy call'. The main motifs of *La mer* are imbued with a quality of incantation, of ancient voices crying out from the depths of the oceans.

Turning now to the movement titles Debussy finally chose, we find Oscar Thompson offering a characteristically vivid explanation of the movements that is excellent prose in itself with some telling hints of how we might elaborate the subject of *La mer*'s programme should we wish to add flesh to the meagre skeleton handed us by Debussy in his movement titles (and overlook his quoted objections to such a literal approach):

De l'aube à midi sur la mer . . . There is a mysterious, eerie quality in the undulations with which this sketch begins. In the music are at once an incantation and an awakening. The chief subject . . . is declaimed by muted trumpet and English horn. Thereafter, as the light seems to grow clearer and Nature more boisterous, the waves of this chimerical sea ride higher, throwing their spume into the sunshine, with all manner of glint and refraction, exultant, tumultuous, but not menacing or cruel. Toward the end, wind instruments intone a solemn and noble theme that has been described as 'the chorale of the depths.' Above it continues the pitching of the waves; there comes a momentary lull, then a last shake of the mane of these horses of the sea.

Jeux de vagues . . . Here Debussy limns his now thoroughly awakened sea at play. There are waves of every color and mood in a capricious sport of wind and spray. . . . The elements dance, they romp and race through immemorial games the secrets of which never will be known to man. The waves become coryphées or they gambol like dolphins. About all is an aura of the remote and the unreal. This is a world of sheer fantasy, of strange visions and eerie voices, a mirage of sight and equally a mirage of sound. On the sea's vast stage is presented a trancelike phantasmagoria so evanescent and fugitive that it leaves behind only the vagueness of a dream.

Dialogue du vent et de la mer . . . presents a gustier and a wilder sea, with a stronger dramatic emphasis and something more closely akin to human quality in the impersonation, however incorporeal it may be, of wind and ocean . . . The dialogue of wind and wave is of cosmic things, of which Debussy's arabesques are cabalistic symbols. The music only hints at the immensities it does not attempt to describe.[20]

This is an altogether fascinating viewpoint, not least for the way it spins a modest narrative across the three movements that may be summarised as 'the sea awakening, the awakened sea at play, the wild sea'. His perception of 'something more closely akin to human quality' in 'Dialogue du vent et de la mer' is pertinent to some of the observations below concerning this movement.

The discarded title of the last movement, 'Le vent fait danser la mer', bears little relation to the character of the present movement, though like the one Debussy finally opted for, it does indicate the presence of two interacting forces. It seems likely that the original title had some significance for Debussy encoded into it that we can only guess at. When the composer wrote to Durand indicating the changed title of the first movement (it is assumed that he also changed the title of the last one at around the same time) there is an ambiguous echo of the discarded title of the finale that cannot be fortuitous: 'there are so many contradictory things dancing around in my head to which this recent flu has added its peculiar dance' (see chapter 2).[21] This was written only two months after the attempted suicide of Lilly and the commentary in his notebook. Is it possible that since the original titles were conceived when Lilly was still in favour, the subsequent changes reflect Emma's ascendancy?

I have mentioned before the possible association of *La mer* with the Poe symphony envisaged but never written in the pre-*Pelléas* days. A further hint comes in Jarocinski's comparison of Monet and Debussy:

Monet's seascapes are never terrifying. We share in the contemplation of the painter, who is himself in a pantheistic harmony with Nature. But in Debussy's *La mer* everything seems to be happening – as with Turner – on a cosmic scale. In the last movement of this polyrhythmic symphony, 'Dialogue du vent et de la mer', the sinister noise of the hurricane seems to portend death and destruction; the same impression is conveyed by the Seventh Prelude (Book I): 'Ce qu'a vu le vent de l'Ouest'.[22]

The mention of Turner implies a crucial element in Poe: terror. This is surely the expressive import of the opening of 'Dialogue du vent et de la mer'. We can compare this music in *La mer*, which seems to stand perilously on the brink of apocalyptic events – catastrophic or otherwise, with the realisation of the calamity that brings the suspense and terror to a grim final outcome in Debussy's sketches for an opera based on *The Fall of the House of Usher*. Usher and his friend are closeted together in a room, disturbed or rather terrified by distant noises that seem to reinforce passages in a book the friend is reading aloud from. A violent tempest accompanies the agonising wait endured by the two men:

A whirlwind had apparently collected its force in our vicinity; for there were frequent and violent alterations in the direction of the wind; and the exceeding density of the clouds (which hung so low as to press upon the turrets of the house) did not prevent our perceiving the lifelike velocity with which they flew careering from all points against each other . . .

For 'the end of the H-U', Debussy includes some of the few instrumental markings in his sketches, namely tam-tam, bass drum and cymbals – the same percussion ensemble playing at the opening of 'Dialogue du vent et de la mer'. A recurrent motif in the sketches, including this crucial moment in the drama, also has parallels with III/9ff, and more obviously with the recall of the first cyclic motif in III/215, completing what seems to be a remarkable reminiscence of a significant part of *La mer*.[23] It hardly seems possible for Debussy to have drawn on this material without there being an expressive correspondence (see Ex. 10).

The extreme violence, the insurmountable and unstoppable energy of *La*

Ex. 10 sketch for *The Fall of the House of Usher* and III/215–17

mer's closing section have strong parallels with the end of the Usher story. The density of Poe's writing increases, obtaining an almost intolerable momentum as a mixture of guilt and terror finally obtain their dreadful pay-off as Usher's sister, inadvertently buried alive by the friends (the deliberation behind this on Usher's part is stronger in Debussy's reworking of the story), crashes into the room and falls heavily upon Usher, killing him. The house falls apart in a *Götterdämmerung*-like conflagration as the friend flees.[24]

Given the sexual adventure Debussy was embarking upon, it may seem strange that Poe should have been on his mind (if it is accepted that he was) as he wrote *La mer*, so perhaps one should interpret *La mer* in a more overtly sexual way and leave aside the Poe symphony reading (the sea has often been associated with sexuality). In fact, Usher and the sexual theme go together, for Debussy's reading of the tale draws on elements only hinted at in the story, Poe himself being little interested in his characters' sexual motivation except in the most indirect way. In his libretto for the proposed opera, Debussy explicitly made Usher's incestuous interest in his sister the reason for the turn events take; sexual inadequacy is only one of several possible explanations for Usher's nervous, wasting 'disease' (a strange condition in Poe that has been much speculated upon). So Debussy had found a sexual theme in the story, a potent one involving Usher's incestuous desire for his sister. Debussy's relationship with Emma was not incestuous, but guilt and fear at the consequences of his actions can only have been overwhelmingly palpable emotions for him.

Poe connections are less easily discerned in movements 1 and 2. As I suggest in chapter 2, it is conceivable that part at least of the finale was sketched or thought of much earlier than the rest of *La mer*, perhaps even around the time Debussy is supposed to have been working on the Poe symphony (1890), hence

Ex. 11   Wagner, *Götterdämmerung*, Act III (Immolation); Valhalla motif

Ex. 12   III/129–35

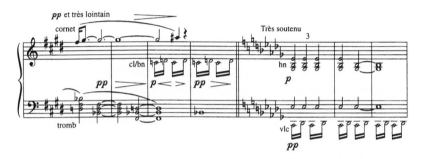

the Franckian character of the principal theme. So one element of 'Dialogue du vent et de la mer' may be an offshoot of that project. Debussy occasionally looks out from his writhing sea to the musical world without. Allusions to other music are not plentiful, but they are there in such forms as the 'Romantic' false climax in 'Dialogue du vent et de la mer'. These are clues from a composer who placed very little reliance upon programmatic formulas of the sort Strauss might use to signal a pastoral setting or pious monks treading the pilgrimage trail. Such explicit symbols have no place in Debussy's music in general. Debussy did not believe in absolute music, but he also mistrusted portraiture, so his works lie midway between, encouraging neither abstract analysis nor straightforward story telling. Even so, the 'Romantic' climax is an exception, for all that its significance is hard to explain. And so, it may be argued, is the mysterious little passage that precedes the *piano* return of the chorale at III/133. Here, I believe, Debussy is making the most oblique reference to the music he had been so satisfyingly exposed to a few months before he started work on *La mer* in London. This is *Götterdämmerung* transformed into a subtle allusion, first to the descending augmented triads that accompany Brünnhilde's ride into the fire, their

43

dynamic character inverted, to be followed by the chorale of Valhalla itself –
as in the opera a few bars later – in the guise of the second cyclic motif (both
are centred on D♭). Debussy found his life devoured by his liaison with Emma;
his friends deserted him and the world turned its back. Here, for a few bars
that might go unnoticed, he makes an ironic, entirely characteristic aside that
is structurally justified (the 'Golliwog's Cakewalk' allusions to *Tristan* are just
as well integrated into their surroundings). This point fits in with other
observations of the expressive character of the finale. Like the Hall of the
Gibichung in *Götterdämmerung*, the House of Usher collapses under the
weight of the tenants' guilt and ignominy at the end, but unlike the Usher
story, a new era is born based on a world redeemed by love through
Brünnhilde's self-sacrifice. Now Debussy mistrusted Wagner's grandilo-
quence and would doubtless have been profoundly reluctant to make too
specific a parallel in *La mer*, but might he not have drawn these worlds together
in a covert way in this, his most important and arguably most personal
orchestral work?

5

Genre and style

Genre

Composers in France and Belgium rising to the challenge of the great revival of orchestral and instrumental music in the last decades of the nineteenth century found their energies divided between programme music, whose main representative was Liszt (Strauss's symphonic poems were gradually appearing in Paris), and 'absolute' music represented by the symphony, sonata, and string quartet. Franck, a crucial figure in the renaissance, evinces this dualism, opting in a number of works for the Lisztian symphonic poem and in others for his distinctive adaptation of the symphony or symphonic chamber work. Few French or Belgian composers – the countries' musical cultures were closely related – accepted the symphony in its Beethovenian form: Franck's cyclic model was preferred, often in three movements; but the symphony was still the ultimate musical ideal, one that was supposed to make the greatest musical demands on both composer and audience.

In the decade of *La mer*, Vincent d'Indy, founder of the Schola Cantorum, composed two multi-movement works that show how one composer could migrate across the divide sketched above. His Second Symphony (composed in 1902–3 and first performed in 1904) pays homage to the ideals of absolute music; its four movements fairly groan under the cyclic principle as motifs are explored and developed, often at great length. Its virtual antithesis, *Jour d'été à la montagne*, followed one year later in 1905. D'Indy described this symphonic triptych in terms that recall aspects of *La mer*: 'These are impressions of my mountain representing three periods of time, *Aurora* (a sunrise without clouds), *Daytime* (a reverie in a pine-wood, with songs coming from down below on the road) and *Evening*.' Its structure is more informal than *La mer*'s. Its opening presents no strongly motivic statement; instead, there are widely-spaced octaves, sonorously scored, which are soon accompanying birdsong. In contrast to *La mer*, a work that refuses to go back on itself, the closing pages of the Finale revert to the initial state of the opening

45

movement, reversing its order so the work dies away on the octave preceded by the hoot of an owl that replaces the other birdsong. In spite of the obvious differences, not least d'Indy's indebtedness to the traditional feeding grounds of French music – Liszt, Wagner, and Franck – *Jour d'été* 'shares with Debussy's seascape its basis in the changing moods and lights of day'.[1]

After a youthful foray (see chapter 1), the mature Debussy exempted himself from the symphony as abstract music. But it is misleading to imply that he took the other path, that of the Lisztian symphonic poem. No such division existed for him. The symphony as practised by Franck's followers was an awful orthodoxy that robbed music of expression and freedom; it was three or four movements into which one poured one's ideas so as to come out with second subjects and development sections. Debussy's irritation with the academic manifestations of the symphony fomented by the d'Indy group was forcibly expressed on several occasions, for example: 'Must we conclude that despite so many attempts at transformation, the symphony – in all its elegance and formal order, and despite its serious-minded bejewelled public – is a thing of the past? Has not its worn-out gilt merely been replaced by a plating of shining copper?'[2] He was no more enamoured of the symphonic poem, whose traditions seemed to involve a subservience to external considerations.

Whereas Debussy poured scorn on the symphonies of many of his French-speaking contemporaries (the Germans rarely entered his consciousness), some Russian specimens were acceptable, especially Rimsky-Korsakov's *Antar* (1869), which is praised for sending the 'traditional form of the symphony packing'.[3] At the time of the composition of *La mer* he also seems to have had unbounded enthusiasm for *Sheherazade* (1888), witnessed in 1903 by Colette in one of the most evocative portraits of Debussy the musician: 'He made humming noises with his lips and reedy ones through his nose to try and recapture a phrase on the oboe, and recreated the timpani's low taps by drumming on the lid of the boudoir grand . . . To imitate a pizzicato on the double-basses, he stood up, took hold of a cork and rubbed it against the window-pane.'[4] Three years later he was off *Sheherazade*, branding it 'more bazaar than oriental'.[5]

There are a substantial number of nineteenth-century multi-movement works that were not symphonic enough to merit the title symphony, sonata, or string quartet, but which still conform in many ways to the attributes of these genres. These works are often known by movement titles, such as Schumann's *Overture, Scherzo and Finale*, Op. 52 (1841/r. 1845), which is remarkably close in scale to *La mer*; the three movements might well have suited a symphony. There are also three-movement works of similar dimensions to *La mer* by Franck, including the piano works *Prélude, choral et fugue* in B minor (1884) and *Prélude, aria et finale* in E major (1886–7), both sturdy examples of the cyclic principle.

Debussy defies rigid classification. He had not composed an orthodox symphony, but neither did he want *La mer* to be known as a symphonic poem (Durand, however, referred to it as 'Debussy's beautiful symphonic poem'), so he chose the subtitle 'Three symphonic sketches'. With these words this inherently non-conforming composer must have felt that he had deftly avoided association with either genre. 'Symphonic' meant anything worked out according to the musical imperatives of motivic and tonal development. His use of the term might well have been a swipe at both his supporters and critics who either revelled in or despised the alleged invertebrate informality of *L'après-midi*, *Nocturnes*, and *Pelléas*.

For all Debussy's posturing, *La mer* comes surprisingly close to the rhetorical and generic characteristics of the nineteenth-century symphony. Formally remote from tradition, the first movement denies recapitulation its accustomed place in the grand scheme of things; yet there is a slow introduction, mysterious and with muted musical focus, which leads into a faster section by means of an *accelerando*. The slow introduction was beloved by Franck and d'Indy among other French symphonists; d'Indy's Second Symphony has one in both first and last movements. Among nineteenth-century symphonies that adopt both a slow introduction and an *accelerando* into the main allegro, Schumann's Fourth offers a fascinating precedent for *La mer* in its first movement. Schumann defies many of the textbook models of sonata form by adopting a progressive scheme for the sonata allegro, incorporating extensive new material into the development section, and making only scanty reference to the exposition in the tersely compressed recapitulation.[6] In addition, Debussy availed himself of another favourite of the French School, the chorale. In d'Indy's Second Symphony the 'fugue which forms the main body of the [last] movement culminates in the usual chorale, the victorious affirmation of positive faith, whose struggles with negation provide the programme of every large-scale work issuing from Franck's circle'.[7] *La mer* ends noisily with a chorale and assertive affirmations of the tonic.

An ambivalent rapprochement with the nineteenth-century symphony is also apparent in 'Jeux de vagues', which recalls the traditional scherzo in character and title. And the finale, an entirely individual structure, nevertheless exploits a prominent, lyrical main theme whose treatment harks back to the example of the Russians, notably Tchaikovsky, especially when the theme is restated by octave strings with pulsating accompaniment in the 'Romantic' climax (see chapter 6). In this, as in other respects, Debussy cast a sympathetic eye over his inheritance, and in so doing penetrated more deeply into the workings of symphonic structure than the composers who regarded unity as guaranteed once a cyclic motif had been heard in each part. Given the complex route that led to his success, epitomised by *La mer's* grand-slam conclusion, it is no wonder he despised most of the symphonies of his day.[8]

Sources of *La mer's* musical style

Provided one is not frightened of generalisation, for present purposes we can trace four levels of influence on *La mer*. The most immediate – and the level most often cited – is the instantly recognisable trace of one composer upon another, such as Wagner lapsing into Liszt's *Faust-Symphonie* in Act II of *Walküre*. *La mer* is almost free from this sort of influence, the most obvious trace being that of Franck, whose imprint is clearly discernible in the principal theme of the last movement. The opening motif of his Piano Quintet (1888–9) pivots around one note and expands in chromatic steps away from it. There is also a reminiscence of the *Rheingold* prelude in the introduction to the first movement.

The second level of influence covers those features not immediately identifiable with one composer, though the distinction with the above category is sometimes a fine one. These involve musical water figures, depictions of the wind and so on, many of which are part of a common coinage that would have been available to any composer wishing to evoke the sea. The arabesque-like flute motif in I/47 is typical; Rimsky-Korsakov uses similar shapes in *Sheherazade*, especially in the sensuous solo-violin motif first heard early on in the first movement.[9] To this we might add the 'thematic relations between the first and last movements [that] parallel somewhat the return of the brass chorale motif in the third movement of Debussy's work'.[10] It is difficult to know what to make of II/231–6, where he almost quotes from *Rigoletto*, a work he does not mention in his writings, and whose composer he was fairly intolerant of. The figure in Ex. 13 is remarkably similar to the off-stage chorus that evokes the storm and Gilda's impending murder in Act III of the opera; yet one cannot say whether this an example of Verdi's influence – it seems unlikely – or simply Debussy's appropriation of a standard icon for the depiction of a storm. Apart from this and the undulating figure (I/31) discussed above, for much of *La mer* Debussy spurns the more obvious devices

48

Ex. 13   II/231–2

associated with the sea, wind, and concomitant storm in favour of his own, highly individual vocabulary.

For the third category we plumb a deeper level of musical experience to unravel the structural origins of a work or composer. The formal outline of *La mer* at first sight seems utterly distinctive: Jean Barraqué adopted the term 'open form' for Debussy's works from *La mer* onwards. However, return to the *Ring* or *Tristan* and consider the music without the words, as the 'bleeding chunks' allow us to do, and we encounter models that might well have influenced Debussy, for nowhere else does one find the improvisatory flexibility that Debussy displays in each movement. Wagner's open-ended formal patterns coincide with Debussy's to a remarkable extent (Wagner's imposition of the symphonic style onto drama had the negative effect, in Debussy's view, of 'killing dramatic music rather than saving it', hence his rejection of it in *Pelléas*).[11] At a harmonic level too Debussy takes off from *Tristan*: the stock of chords is similar, though the resemblance is confined to their taxonomy. Whereas Wagner makes his enriched harmonic palette follow roughly the principles of voice leading and directed, cadential bass motion that Beethoven would have recognised, Debussy does not.

The fourth level of influence covers the effect of an aesthetic or school upon a composer rather than elements of musical language. This is the area in which Debussy was more likely to find himself outside the sphere of musical influence altogether, given his predilection for literary company and suspicion of musicians. Nevertheless, in spite of the differences that existed between them, Debussy remained subliminally attached to Franck as a kind of father figure to be admired rather than emulated; his influence is present in *La mer*. Perhaps the mixed feelings he felt towards this venerated figure were due to the fact that although he spent much of his life in opposition to the school founded in his name by d'Indy, he was comfortably ensconced in the Société Nationale, which brought him into regular contact with those very composers whose practices he so often condemned (see chapter 1). Perhaps then he defined himself through a negative, and thence to a liberated view of music:

escape from the Schola Cantorum's way of doing things spelt freedom for him. It is also likely that unconventional works like Lalo's colourful ballet *Namouna* (1874), which so flamboyantly flouted the system, had as strong an impact on Debussy's development as Franck. It was received by him with such boisterous enthusiasm, he was ejected from the theatre. *La mer* represents both the conservative and progressive strains in Debussy's background.

6

Design

Formal structure

Complimentary and uncomplimentary charges of radical informality and amorphousness have always greeted Debussy's works. Climaxes that dissolve almost before they have begun and whose function does not seem designed to signpost a clear point of formal departure, such as a recapitulation, have been viewed as essential qualities of both Debussy's style and the Impressionist movement in music. Commentators still speak of Debussy's music as nebulous, ill-defined, and so on – a music carried on the wake of dreams. Schoenberg, evidently swayed by the Impressionist label, described Debussy's harmonies (he might as well have been referring to form) as 'without constructive meaning, [which] often served the colouristic purpose of expressing moods and pictures. Moods and pictures, though extra-musical, thus became constructive elements, incorporated in the musical functions; they produced a sort of emotional comprehensibility.'[1]

It is salutary to consider that ill-defined formal boundaries are not a ubiquitous part of Debussy's compositional style so much as a resource available to him. They are most remarkable in *L'après-midi* where a latent ABA division is skilfully masked; the 'parts seem to overlap each other, so that the continuity of the whole work is extraordinarily smooth, and our recollection of it at the end is imprecise, though intense'.[2] This work has done more to shape the popular perception of Debussy's style than any other, yet it is no more reasonable to use it to define the whole of his output than it would be to define Beethoven's symphonic style on the basis of the Fifth Symphony. As William Austin remarks, the veiled formal divisions of *L'après-midi* recall an important characteristic of the poem, so they have a specific function. There is therefore no reason why he should have maintained this characteristic of *L'après-midi*, carelessly labelled Impressionistic (ignoring its Symbolist source), in *La mer*.

'De l'aube à midi sur la mer' is formally the opposite of the *L'après-midi*.

Its formal boundaries are crystal clear: at four moments in the movement new material is introduced that is a pronounced departure from anything preceding it: witness the cello theme of bars 84ff. The ends of the two principal sections fade away into obscurity, but that merely emphasises the strength of the new beginning that follows. On the other hand, the formal pattern that these clearly differentiated sections produce, ABCDE (!), does not remotely recall a textbook norm; *L'après-midi* does.[3]

Only the third movement seems to adhere to an orthodox scheme; its clear formal divisions resemble rondo form, and there are those who find a manifestation of sonata form in it; but the way two thematic groupings change character and function in the movement makes the comparison with either hard to sustain.

'Jeux de vagues', like *Jeux*, is taken as a landmark in the dissolution of formal boundaries in favour of a vague openness, the music spinning out its course according to the whims of the tone painter like the arabesques that flowed from the brush of the *art nouveau* or Impressionist painter. In an influential essay Herbert Eimert claims Debussy as a precursor of post-war electro-acoustic music as it was practised in Cologne in the 1950s:

Debussy's handling of form is a withdrawal – he reduces to it the movement of ornaments, motifs and flocculi . . . the hidden impetus of the current creates a new organic coherence, that of flowing form, an ornamental kinetic form which makes the cellular plan and line-by-line structure of the four-bar phrase so supple that they can freely follow the vibration of the form and can themselves become flexible form.

Eimert places great emphasis on the perceived absence of development in Debussy, suggesting that he had rejected all manner of rhetoric in the continuation of his themes, especially the type of melodic structure referred to as antecedent–consequent.[4] *Jeux* is undoubtedly more extreme in this matter than 'Jeux de vagues', but Eimert is overstating his case even for *Jeux* when he claims that 'in the vegetative circulation of the form there is no development, no intensification or return of themes'. In *La mer* motifs are constantly propagated by derivation from earlier motifs, and repetition becomes increasingly important as the work proceeds. Nevertheless, whilst there are moments of recapitulation, often muted, in 'Jeux de vagues', an unprecedented level of exposition of new material, or material only loosely derived from previous motivic elements, hints suggestively at Eimert's 'vegetative circulation of the form'.

A valuable corrective to the Impressionist interpretation of Debussy's forms comes in Howat's *Debussy in Proportion*, which claims that the formal boundaries are based upon Golden Section and other proportional means.[5] In parts of the outer movements in particular, analysis reveals spirals based on GS, and Howat cites as evidence the suppression of one bar in the first movement (see chapter 2), which results in keeping the 'percentage inaccuracy' of GS to a minimum. The precise significance of these findings is hard to assess, but the intrinsic evidence is remarkable; there is, however, no material proof (letters, sketches, anecdotes, for example) – other than the finished works – that Debussy consciously contrived such proportional schemes.

In the synopsis that follows, a table showing the basic formal elements of each movement is followed by a commentary that deals selectively with some of the numerous 'currents' running through *La mer*.

Synopsis

Movement I: 'De l'aube à midi sur la mer'

Textbooks on form offer us little enlightenment in the face of a movement as unusual as this. To claim that it fulfils the requirements of sonata form on account of its bithematicism and movement away from and back to D♭ is surely stretching the term beyond any reasonable tolerance. Ansermet, a notable conductor of Debussy, recognised this when he wrote that this movement has 'all the allure of a symphonic allegro, of sonata form' and 'it fulfils the *tonal* conditions of the form as well, but its content is quite different to an allegro in a classical symphony. It is quite different, above all, because Debussy does not develop themes . . . If he repeats the first motif three times it is to show it in a new light and base an argument on it . . . With Debussy the music is always moving on without going back on itself.'[6] In the brilliantly-lit coda a new motif of considerable importance (the second cyclic motif) is introduced, so extending the principle of continual exposition through to the last moment. Running in harness with the exposition of new ideas is a distinctive developmental process involving the absorption of certain features of one unit in the next. This rarely recalls orthodox developmental patterns (found in abundance in d'Indy's music, for example). These two factors – exposition and development – prompted Barraqué to describe this movement as the first example of 'open form': 'In *La mer* Debussy invented a procedure of development in which the notions of exposition and development co-exist in an uninterrupted stream, permitting the work to be propelled along by itself without recourse to any pre-established model.'[7]

Table 2. *Formal structure of 'De l'aube à midi sur la mer'*

		progressive/open form	8:32	D♭
1	introduction	arch	0:00	B
31	first principal section	arch	1:21	D♭>E
84	second principal section	variations	4:34	C/B♭
122	interlude	strophic (a, a¹)	6:39	
132	coda	progressive	7:25	D♭

The first movement falls into five clear-cut sections based on an introduction, two sharply contrasted principal sections, and a coda separated from these sections by a short interlude imbued with its own motivic identity (Satie liked a moment in this movement before 'a quarter to 11' – this is surely it).[8] Within each section there is some repetition, little of it literal, which produces various ternary, arch, refrain, and other forms. The timings in the fourth column of Table 2 are based on Karajan's 1964 DG recording.[9]

I/1–30: introduction

Cox writes, 'the opening music symbolises pentatonically the sun rising in the East', so conveying the impression that we are at the beginning of a narrative based on time passing, one that is to culminate in the radiant vision of the midday sun in the movement's coda.[10] At the opening our sense of time is misty, undefined as the harps echo each other without establishing a regular pulse. From the depths of the orchestra over a pedal B, mysterious pentatonic figures rise up in the middle strings, tentatively marking out the tonal space. Two motivic events follow at close intervals, first a turning figure introduced by a semiquaver–dotted quaver appoggiatura figure (Ex. 14) – derivatives of this are to be among the most widely used motifs in the work – and then a 'melancholy call, in an instant summoning up the kingdom of the wind to our gaze' (Ex. 15).[11] This 'call' is the first cyclic motif and marks the apex of an arch, after which we work backwards through the motifs to the first principal section.

The term 'arch form' does not convey the introduction's inner dynamic, which is weighted towards the *accelerando* of the final part (bar 23) that launches the *Modéré sans lenteur* at bar 31. The tonality is obscure; although emphasis on B in the bass and later in the treble gives some sense of stability, the lack of any cadential progression and such contradictory events as the fixation of the first cyclic motif on C make even this tenuous.

Ex. 14   motif *x*, I/6–9

motif *x*

Ex. 15   first cyclic motif, I/12–17

I/31–83: first principal section

Like the second principal section, this part of the movement is to a high degree autonomous, evolving and developing its own material based on a mode founded on D♭ (variously labelled acoustic scale or *Vachaspati* acoustic scale), and later transposed to E.[12] Formally this section is a free adaptation of the arch form of the introduction, with some elements of the first part omitted or rearranged after the central episode.

For two bars we hear an elaborate polyphony of accompanimental figures. Their definition of a D♭ major triad is obscured by the trilling figure in the second violins which continually places E♭ and B♭ over the triad; for this reason, one can barely speak of the section as being triadically based at all; instead, we find one pitch, D♭, receiving strong reinforcement from harps and bassoons. There is consequently a rather nebulous quality to the harmony that is reflected in other domains as well, though the overriding impression is of an inexorable surge founded upon three layers of semiquaver or semiquaver-triplet figures that spread into other motivic areas after the original ostinato of bars 31–42 has ceased.

Over the flowing accompaniment, diverse motivic material is presented in spurts, building every so often to a short-lived climax from which events rapidly decay and return to the muted dynamics prevalent in this section. The first motif, a terse pentatonic one in fifths (Ex. 16), contrasts strongly with the second, a long-breathed horn motif (Ex. 17). As a gesture, the horns' motif is a remote descendant of the first cyclic motif, most obviously in its octave registration, which replaces the cyclic motif's trumpet/cor anglais instrumen-

Ex. 16   I/33

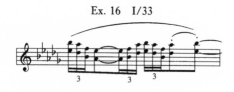

Ex. 17   I/35–7

tation with the bracing sound of four horns. Slight parallels between the motifs account for the uncanny feeling that the horn motif is at once familiar and unfamiliar, as so often happens in *La mer*.

The extended phrase length of the horn motif is replaced by the rapid alternation in one-bar units of the pentatonic figure and a new motif strikingly scored for oboe, harp, and solo cello in octaves; the initial orchestral colouring is inseparable from the idea and imprints itself firmly on the mind. Like waves lapping against the side of a boat, ideas come and go in the first part of the arch without creating the structural tension that would generate a turning point in the music, the type of escalating exchange of ideas that Wagner would employ to prefigure a new dramatic departure in *Tristan*, for example. But as the section proceeds, short anacrustic gestures begin to appear that are born out of the kinetic energy of the one-bar exchanges. The first of these is just one bar (bar 46); its ability to make a structural connection across the bar is limited, for the ensuing motif, a new one, largely ignores the voice-leading or other implications of this upbeat bar.

The new motif in bar 47 is more arabesque-like than any we have heard so far (Ex. 18). A sensuous flute melody in semiquaver triplets languorously recalls *Sheherazade*'s erotically-charged violin solo. The chordal accompaniment is new too, as is the dissonant harmony which places a semitone over the minor triad (the same dissonance Beethoven used to depict chaos in his Ninth Symphony). The motif is repeated straightaway with some variation, leading at bar 51 to an extended return of the anacrustic figure of bar 46. Dynamics remain low, but there is a sense of greater excitement, of a suppressed energy that has to be unleashed.

The horn motif returns in bar 53 with a new accompaniment evolved with

Ex. 18   I/47–8

seeming inevitability from the start of the first principal section. As well as the feather-light tremolos in the upper strings, the basses pluck a rising arpeggio figure which is one of several manifestations of the changing harmonic environment in which the untransposed horn motif finds itself. The new harmonies involve a transposition of the mode from D♭ to E.

A slight dip in the basic tempo brings a poignant moment as a solo violin adds a melancholy counterpoint to an oboe's minor-third motif in bar 59. This is the centre of the arch and a moment of reflection, a foil to the reckless intensity of the surrounding music. It is followed with very little attempted connection by the arabesque motif (Ex. 18), transposed down a minor third, and harmonised with a less dissonant harmony. From this point, the anacrustic attempts of bars 46 and 51–2 begin to enter the broader canvas after their confinement in a pointillist manner to individual bars; against overlapping statements of the horn motif (again at its original pitch) and first cyclic motif (bar 72), the music builds to a series of repeated registral and dynamic peaks at the rate of once a bar. Thrown into this excitable fray is the pentatonic motif (Ex. 16), which now becomes just one more element in a complex contrapuntal texture.

At the completion of the arch, motivic elements are liquidated – the first cyclic motif's reappearance in bar 72 therefore comes at a moment of atrophy rather than climactic articulation in the manner of Franck's cyclic works. This is perpetuated in the second principal section.

I/84–121: second principal section

This is a bold new beginning in every sense. Cellos (and other strings) have played only an accompanying role so far; now a new motif (Ex. 19) is played by four desks of them (a moment to be dreaded in a performance, so rarely do they play in tune). The whole musical environment is altered with a new tempo, fresh articulation, and a B♭ major key signature with attention focused on C as a latent tonic, hence the Dorian-mode feel.

Debussy increases the tempo after two bars as the cello theme is repeated

Ex. 19 I/86–8

and greatly extended, producing a five-bar phrase with a contour that peaks in bar 89 (this is not repeated in its entirety). Sixteen cellos are called for, a number that few orchestras outside the luxurious confines of the Berlin Philharmonic can afford – hence the legitimate use of viola reinforcements (not, one hastens to add, playing at the octave as they sometimes do). There is a great feeling of elation in this passage, especially when it is played at the brisk tempo marked (crotchet = 104). The propensity of the cello motif to climax on two oscillating notes with the rhythm ♪ ♪. ♪ recalls the physical impact of a boat rocking from side to side, and makes a tentative motivic connection with the violins in bars 31ff.

The second principal section is organised as two variations on the cello theme (bars 98, 105) with the variations linked by interludes of mounting intensity; they are followed by a long passage of dwindling momentum. Each variation shortens the original theme, at the same time adding to the dynamic level and excitement. At the culmination of the second variation the head motif of the cello theme is repeated twice as the dynamic ebbs rapidly away. Tonal focus is soon lost as we part company with the two-flat key signature and turn to whole-tone scales based on C♯ in bar 109 and C in bar 110, heard for the first time in *La mer*.

As the harmonic mist descends, a new version of the first cyclic motif is heard from muted trumpet in bar 112. Fragments of other motifs discretely appear in the wind as strings maintain a rocking ostinato figure derived from the cello theme. The rising tritone motif that grows out of the whole-tone harmony is only loosely connected with previous motifs; yet it does not sound unfamiliar (perhaps because the filled-in fourth forms part of the first cyclic motif).[13] This same tritone, now falling, is incorporated into the interlude that follows in bar 122 (see Ex. 20), and various manifestations of it figure prominently elsewhere in *La mer* (the first, incomplete, entry of the first cyclic motif in I/9 is on C against the oboe's F♯, and the first cyclic motif itself has A♭–D in its fourth bar).

A reduction in tempo works alongside the liquidation of harmonic and motivic elements in the second principal section. By the end, proceedings are

Ex. 20   I/115, 122–5

well and truly becalmed; so much so that it is easy to overlook the arrival of A♭ in the bass in bar 122, the pitch that might automatically be marked out as the dominant of D♭ major were Debussy's harmony functioning traditionally.[14]

I/122–31 interlude

The whole-tone harmonies of the closing stages of the second principal section linger on in the pile of thirds above the A♭ (retained from the interlude) that *looks* like an altered dominant thirteenth (!), but Debussy deprives it of any dominant function by skilful registration and by not resolving the dissonances within it. When the next section begins on a G♭ major triad, we do not get the sense of a resolution of the 'dominant' harmony, or progression from one harmony to another, so much as a transformation of the 'dominant thirteenth' into the G♭ triad by shifting pitches by a tone or a semitone (in the string parts B♭ is retained while D♮ moves to D♭ and A♭ to G♭). Debussy's alchemy changes what looks like a dominant–subdominant progression in D♭ major (a mortal sin in harmony textbooks) into a harmonic example of 'vegetative circulation' (see page 52).

This ten-bar section is based on two strophes of four bars with only minor variations in the second, and a two-bar extension. Momentum here is slack; the sea has become uneventful.

I/132–end: coda

As the A♭ in the bass drops to G♭ for the beginning of the coda, there is a tremendous sense of looming power as the trombones make their first entry in *La mer*. The chorale or 'call of the deep', the second cyclic motif, symbolises the midday sun bursting through the sea mist after the stillness and passivity of the interlude. It is not quite a motivic novelty: the rhythm of the first four notes is (proportionally) the same as that of the first cyclic motif, though other attributes make it a striking example of Debussy's use of exposition right up to the final moments of the movement. Heard against it are reverberations of the woodwind's pentatonic motif from the first principal section (Ex. 16), and

59

a modified version of motif *x* of bars 6–9 (see Ex. 14). In spite of the vast swell of sound, the ending is abrupt and we are allowed to hear an unadorned D♭ major triad – the first – for just four crotchets as it dies rapidly away.

Although 'De l'aube à midi sur la mer' returns to the D♭ key signature in the interlude, D♭ major's definition as a tonic is tenuous – witness the way B♭ is held above the final chord for two crotchets. The strength of the final cadence is as much due to the assertiveness of the motivic gesture E♭–D♭–B♭, which parallels the climax of the first principal section at bar 76 (C♯–B–G♯), as to a resolution of the first movement's harmonic issues. There is consequently unfinished business to be addressed in the next two movements, both of which take up the B♭ in different ways. It is not until the last movement that the D♭ major triad becomes securely identified as a tonic harmony detached from its sixth (see chapter 7).

Movement II: 'Jeux de vagues'

There are some points on which writers on *La mer* will never reach agreement; of them all, the form of 'Jeux de vagues' is probably the most vexing, for it bears only a cursory correspondence to nineteenth-century norms. Max Pommer in his preface to the Peters score described it as ternary with an introduction, but placed beside any movement of *Nocturnes* (where ternary forms are the norm) there is an astonishing 'advance' in formal complexity. This is reflected in Howat's alternative two-fold binary scheme ('overlapping binary systems') in which consideration of motivic and tonal repetition yields two formal layers:

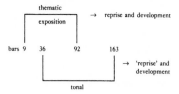

This is one of many attempts at defining this movement, and though its recognition of a disjunction between motivic and tonal forms is intriguing, it is unconvincing: the part described as a tonal exposition is as much a motivic one; similarly, the events described as motivic also participate in a tonal process, one that gradually brings musical events into orbit around E. The differentiation between tonal and motivic events seems, therefore, arbitrary.[15]

Douglass Green expressed dissatisfaction with any type of formal or schematic classification, suggesting instead that we 'abandon the traditional concepts of statement, development, and restatement [and listen] to the work as a coherent flow of short moments merging from one to the next'.[16] This view is similar to one expressed by Laurence Berman who noted how events on the way to the climax of 'Jeux de vagues' set 'up an alternation of impediments and forward impulses, before the final forward sweep towards *38* [bar 163] gets properly under way'.[17]

Rather than adapting the various explanations that have come forward, an unappealing task, I have attempted to go with the grain of the movement by identifying four principal stages. Motivic recapitulation seems incidental to the open form of the first two parts, so I have not reflected Howat's thematic returns in the partition. Part 1 (Pommer's introduction) comprises three sections, the last of which produces an upbeat to the tonal and motivic 'exposition' that begins Part 2. Part 2 echoes Part 1 in one attribute, namely the way its closing stages develop an (extended) upbeat to the return of Part 2's opening tonal and motivic material in Part 3. The level of intensity and breadth of statement has been transformed, however. From Part 3 to the end, events occur on a broader scale; local pulls and pushes, to paraphrase Berman, give way to an all-consuming forward motion that reaches an *fff* climax and then rapidly subsides into Part 4.[18] This final part better suits the title 'coda' than the first part 'introduction', which fails to encompass the expository and other processes working in Part 1. In contrast, the final section is primarily cadential in function and therefore has much in common with what is usually meant by 'coda'.

The first two parts are divided into several shorter sections, each identifiable by new or partly new motivic content. Indicative of the transformation that occurs in the last two sections is the fact that they are perceived as wholes without these multifarious subdivisions. The right-hand column of Table 3 refers to the subdivisions, not motifs; but I have taken the opportunity to show where the main material of a section is based on returning material, as in bars 118–23, which combine elements of sections A, B, and I.

II/1: Part 1

Two two-bar phrases based on hushed string tremolos, a sustained wind chord, and delicate splashes of colour in the glockenspiel and harps hint at sustained motion that is crushed when flutes enter in bar 4 with a sinuous, chromatic figure which is taken up by the clarinets in a kind of reverberation.

Table 3. *Formal structure of 'Jeux de vagues'*

Movement II			progressive/open	6:10	>E	
Part 1:	1		bar aab	0:00		A
	9		strophic a, a¹	0:13		B
	28		bar	0:35	>B♭V⁹	C
Part 2:	36			0:45	E	D
	48			1:00		E
	60		bar	1:16		F
	72			1:36		G
	82			1:51		H
	92	motivic returns		2:07	A	A/I[F]
	104	motivic returns	bar	2:27		F
	118	motivic returns		2:49	A	A/B/I
	124	turning point	rondo	2:58		J
	147	build up		3:33	>B♭V⁹	K
Part 3:	163	tonal and motivic return	strophic variation	3:55	E>G♯>B♭V⁹	D/L
Part 4:	219	coda	rondo	5:00	E	B/E/M

(This passage may be interpreted as a depiction of a gull diving into the water in search of food, breaking the calm surface of the water painted in bars 1–4, and sending up spray that is caught up in the wind.)[19] Disparate other sonorities follow, including repeated trumpet notes and string trills, gossamer-like tendrils of sound that give no hint of a tonal centre or motivic direction. Cello and second bassoon delicately adumbrate the cor anglais motif of the next section with their F♯–C tritone.

II/9

The cor anglais' tritone motif follows the two-bar pattern of the opening, maintaining aspects of the first section's texture, including tremolo strings and splashes of colour from harps and glockenspiel. On its repetition in bar 11, this tritone motif runs off into arabesque-like semiquavers which extend the length of the cor anglais' phrase from two to seven bars, though other instrumental details create two- or three-bar subdivisions of this.

A mysterious imprecision in the arabesque is wrought by the use of heterophony in bars 16–17 (flute and cor anglais have the same melodic outline but different rhythmic values; see Ex. 21). Passages of this sort proliferate in 'Jeux de vagues'. At bar 18 the gist of the previous passage (bars 9–17) is repeated, transposed by a tritone; this is a good example of the way a motivic

Ex. 21 II/16

feature – the cor anglais' tritone – moves out from the motivic domain to control harmonic movement.

II/28

This very brief section completes the opening phase of the movement by articulating an upbeat to the more stable section that follows. The primary harmony here, a dominant ninth on B♭, comes to function as a dominant to the harmony on E which, subject to several transformations, becomes increasingly identified as the tonal centre.

Throughout the movement new sections incorporate elements of previous ones; in this section the rising tritone motif is again heard in the cor anglais, but dominating our attention is a forceful three-note figure in the horns and cascading arpeggiations of the dominant ninth in the upper woodwind.

II/36: Part 2

After the upbeat preparation at the end of Part 1, much needed stability endures for twelve bars in Part 2, which is a long time amidst the twists and turns of Parts 1 and 2. For the first time, limited tonal security is offered in the form of a seventh chord built on E that incorporates an augmented fifth (E–B♯) alternating with a perfect fifth (E–B). It supports a similarly stable melody in the violins that seems to be setting out on a regular musical 'sentence' that would comprise a statement, counterstatement bar 40, development bar 44, and closure bar 48.[20] After the first three stages – statement, counterstatement, and development – Debussy decisively pulls the rug out from under us with the harp glissandos at bar 48, abruptly terminating melodic, textural, and most other vestiges of the stable flow of the three foregoing phrases, and denying us local closure.

II/48

Tantalisingly, the bass moves to a B at the beginning of this section. It lingers on for ten bars, supporting whole-tone harmonies that bear a striking resemblance to a dominant ninth on B with the fifth altered from F♯ to F♮.

Ex. 22   II/50–1

Is this a conventional dominant of E major? The sense of disruption is so great in bar 48, the answer is probably 'no': the B is heard as a lone relic of a harmonic order that has yet to define a dominant–tonic relationship (what we have heard so far makes B♭ the more likely dominant, not B). Our attention is consequently focused on whatever motivic events are to follow, which turn out to be remote from bars 36–47 in both contour and timbre, so enforcing the sense that this lone B and its altered 'dominant' harmony have little in common with the E-based harmony preceding it. In the coda the bass returns to this B, which is finally led to E in a strong closing cadence. Much harmonic activity and development is necessary before this transformation can occur; until then, the tritone dominant on B♭ is of greater syntactical importance.

The horn motif introduced at II/50 (see Ex. 22) is the first of a family of motifs based on a ♩. ♪♪♪ or 𝄾 ♩ ♪♪♪, moving away from and back to the starting point in mainly conjunct motion. It represents a more assertive style of melodic construction than the trills and arabesques up to now; this is a style that will eventually lead to the triumphant lyricism that brings this movement to its glowing climax. At this point, however, the development of these motifs is tied to the abrupt changes of direction and texture every two bars that characterise the music of Parts 1 and 2 (until around bar 126).

II/60

Bars 60–1 preface a new motif with its accompaniment alone, so following a fairly common pattern of introducing new motifs with a two-bar phrase. Those who appreciate such things will be pleased by Berman's nickname for this motif, namely 'smooth-sailing'.[21] In motivic terms it is another derivative of the horn motif heard in bar 50. Its character represents a continual aspiration on the part of the music in 'Jeux de vagues' for just that – 'smooth sailing', or a flow of developing material in place of interruptions and deflections. For the moment this remains only an aspiration. In spite of the momentum inherent in the motif, deflection takes place at bar 68 with an abrupt cessation of the repeated chords in flutes and clarinets; the timbre of

Ex. 23   II/76–8

the main melodic voice changes from cor anglais, which holds a privileged position in 'Jeux de vagues', to chordal string texture.

II/72

Even the tentative continuity achieved in the foregoing section is overridden in the swirling demisemiquaver activity of the woodwind and violins. The horn motif, itself new, seems to have a disruptive effect that counteracts the momentum of the 'smooth-sailing' motif. Eventually, new melodic material emerges from the woodwind-violin dialogue; a clarinet motif shyly suggests a fresh motivic formula, to which the horns reply with a figure that ingeniously incorporates the cor anglais' tritone (see Ex. 23).

II/82

This section is separated from the previous one by the cessation of the demisemiquaver activity; it is a motivic offshoot of the clarinet figure of bar 76.

II/92

After a return to the tritone dominant at the end of the previous section (bars 90–1), shimmering textures recall the opening of the movement. The return of the tritone motif marks a turning point in the sense that the endless stream of new material (or transformations of previously stated material) is to be counterbalanced by an element of recapitulation. Within a few bars, however, the return of earlier motifs is interrupted by an expressive episode of great beauty (bars 97–103). Its arrangement here represents a new advance in the continuity of its phrasing and in the use for the first time of model-and-sequence construction, which by its very nature provides congruity and relationship.[22]

II/104

Growing emphasis on recapitulation in 'Jeux de vagues' is maintained as the 'smooth-sailing' motif returns. There is promise here of even greater flow as the motif is repeated and developed; were it not for the change of harmony in bars 112–13, one might be tempted to view the whole section as an antecedent–consequent period. However, flow resulting from this repetition is diffused at II/116 as the texture and rhythmic patterns dissolve.

II/118

Material from the first two sections of Part 1 is merged in bars 118–21. A reprise of bars 95–6 then turns bars 118–23 into a six-bar period structured aab. Were this the end of the sequence, it would form a nicely homogeneous unit, but on the final crotchet a new trumpet motif disrupts the pattern, exercising a breaking action (note how the trumpet is marked *piano, cresc. molto* – a subtlety universally ignored).

II/124

All movement freezes on a dissonant harmony in bar 126, C♯–E♯–G♯–B–A♯, that would, were orthodox influences at work, resolve to a dominant seventh on C♯. Instead, the A♯, repeated by the harps, changes enharmonically to B♭ and is incorporated into a G minor triad with a muted added sixth (E) in bar 130. The arrival of a minor triad here is portentous: we are at an important juncture in the movement with fresh priorities set to take over the ordering of events. It is typical of the way harmonic language evolves and adapts itself to changing circumstances during the three movements of *La mer* that this is the first clear-cut minor triad so far.

From bar 134 a chromatic motif initially given to the first clarinet alternates with the trumpet motif, part of which is repeated twice, so producing a miniature rondo. Although the trumpet motif is but a pale echo of its former self, its regular alternation with the clarinet motif contrasts with the perfunctory schemes heard so far. Rather in the manner of Tchaikovsky, the pace accelerates as two-bar phrases are replaced by a one-bar dialogue between strings and woodwind using variants of the clarinet motif from bar 142. This is the beginning of the metamorphosis of time in 'Jeux de vagues'.

II/147

The clarinet motif is dismissed in the acceleration towards the chords that herald the return at bar 163 of the material that opened Part 2 (bars 36–47), but its semiquaver triplets are retained in whirling string arpeggios (the harmony incorporates the G minor chord with the added major sixth of bars 131ff, inverting it by placing E in the bass). The repeated bass pizzicato line that drives this passage on may at first seem new, but its origin can be traced back to a figure heard just a few bars before: it is an extension of the A♭–B–D bass line of bars 142 and 144. Similarly, the single-bar phrases are reinforced at bar 149 by horn figures that are a distant descendant of the tritone motif. (Debussy's concern that they would not be clearly articulated in performance is shown by the *marqué* articulation and the addition of *en dehors* to the British Library annotated copy of the 1905 score, not acted on in the 1909 edition.)

The imposing chords (bars 153ff) that prepare the return of the material of bars 36–47 in Part 3 combine elements of the whole-tone scale (on C) with the dominant ninth chord on B♭, the tritone dominant. The treble line traces the figure F♯–E–D–C, an inversion of the tritone motif of bar 9.

II/163: Part 3

We now have confirmation of the change in the way time is organised in a passage Berman called 'a rebeginning . . . a huge consequent phrase'.[23] The trill figure and arabesque of bars 36–47 return, but with a difference. Whereas they previously constituted the principal voice (bars 36–9), they are now relegated to the flutes as the first violins project the new time scale by trilling impatiently on the G♯ retained from the end of Part 3; they punctuate their four-bar units with a semiquaver figure in bars 166 and 170. After an eight-bar statement and counterstatement (closely related to the opening eight bars of Part 2), instead of development and interruption, a new motif of four bars duration is introduced in the second violins and cello. It is developed in waves of mounting intensity for the next forty bars. The contrast with Parts 1 and 2 could not be greater. The new motif radiates an ecstatic sense of well being.

As the melody is sustained and developed the bass remains rooted on G♯. It is a paradox of 'Jeux de vagues' that the climax, so long in coming, does not bring with it a confirmation of the E-based harmony that opens Part 3. Nevertheless, G♯ (A♭) is a member of both the tonic triad – as E major is subsequently defined – and the tritone dominant on B♭.

The principal melodic line of Part 3 is devoted exclusively to the new melody introduced at bar 171, which is developed by varied repetition in a conspicuously traditional style. Intensive counterpoint in other voices brings in fragments of many motifs from Parts 1 and 2, including the disruptive trumpet of bar 123 and the tritone motif. None of them possesses the capacity to break the new-found phraseology so securely rooted in four-bar units. At the climactic moment (bar 215), the B♭ dominant ninth returns with the opening of the disruptive trumpet motif. The continuum dramatically disintegrates in bar 219, leaving only broken fragments of the melodic glories of Part 3.

II/219: Part 4

After the return of the B♭ dominant-ninth harmony in bar 215, the continuity of the climactic surge collapses and the coda seems determined to mark a return to diversionary features like the harp glissandos and tritone motif. Debussy's progressive evolution of his musical material does not permit such a retrograde step: cadential motions, particularly in the bass line and arising from the tritone motif, give this entire section a unanimity of purpose that roundly belies any sense of the fragmentation of Parts 1 and 2.

Debussy revised the end of this movement at a late stage in the compositional process; although we do not know what he did to achieve his desire that it be 'neither open nor closed' (see chapter 2), one of the revisions may have been the addition of the chromatic viola/cello figure of bars 231–6, added as a harbinger of the storm that follows in 'Dialogue du vent et de la mer', whose agitated tremolos and chromatic profile it resembles (especially III/9–12).

After an approach to the tonic E major triad that results in the harmony with added sixth (bars 245–50), a plain triad is finally reached – the first – as the rising tritone motif at last reaches B. The triad is still qualified at the end, albeit very lightly, by a C♯ in the glockenspiel. The presence of this C♯ is reminiscent of the added sixth at the close of 'De l'aube à midi sur la mer', but unlike the situation in that movement, where the D♭ triad was confined to a narrow registral area, the three notes of this triad are spread evenly across almost the whole frequency spectrum available to Debussy's orchestra with the fifth prominent on top.

Movement III: 'Dialogue du vent et de la mer'

The sectional précis shown below makes it clear how one might interpret this movement as a rondo given the alternation of a principal theme, which is the main element in the part referred to below as the 'second group' (refrain), and a series of interludes based on a contrasted group of motifs (couplet). Other analysts have found a useful model in sonata form, including Howat who makes the following divisions: introduction; exposition, bar 56; development, bar 157; recapitulation, bar 211; coda, bar 258.[24] The coda is the point at which the chorale returns. The tonal, motivic, or gestural activity in each of these sections makes it hard to endorse this reading. For example, one would expect a development section to be tonally fluid and motivically exploratory, yet here the reverse is true: there is a long lull during which the only harmony heard is that of D♭ major supporting the principal theme; at the climax, after a few bars of tonal uncertainty, there is a full restatement of the principal theme, again in D♭, and almost in its entirety. So the development is not a development in any received sense of the term, and the recapitulation does not mark the point of tonal return; on the contrary, bars 211ff (Howat's recapitulation) are based on vagrant harmonies and present new versions of existing motifs.

As in 'Jeux de vagues', there is a subtle transformational process feeding through from section to section, and it is in many ways more helpful to erase terms like 'recapitulation' so as to appreciate the continuity and variety of the evolutionary process; one would do so in the knowledge that Debussy might be spared yet more gyrations in his grave!

This view was shared by Barraqué who was responsible for some of the most suggestive writing on the structure of 'Dialogue du vent et de la mer'. He describes 'two contrasting forces in the last movement "dialogue": a chaotic, rhythmically-oriented idea, and a singing, melodically-oriented idea . . . a motion from the rhythmic to the melodic element'.[25] In pursuit of his hypothesis, Barraqué may oversimplify matters, missing subtleties on the way, but he conveys the notion of ideas in motion merging from one to the next as functions and characteristics migrate between the two opposing groups of motifs; all this is lost when one becomes overly attached to a segmentation based on a traditional view of form (see Table 4).

III/1: first group, and III/56: second group

'Dialogue du vent et de la mer' opens with menacing, violent music. Debussy rarely expressed terror and foreboding so forthrightly (in *Pelléas* the violence is held on a tighter rein). The tritone that underpins the harmony through the first 44 bars – C–F♯ – is the same one heard in I/9, the interlude (I/122), and throughout 'Jeux de vagues'.

The presence of two dramatically contrasted thematic groups creates a dialectic or dichotomy that becomes the substance of the movement and brings to the surface conflicts between periodic melody and more volatile elements latent in the two previous movements. In the first section, the first cyclic motif plays a decisive role; Laloy's 'melancholy call' (see page 39) is transformed into a 'call to arms', a warning or challenge; this is enhanced by its association with brass sonorities. That it might also depict the wind of the movement's title is suggested by the string tremolos that accompany it in bar 38 when we hear orchestral figures that are more explicitly referential than almost any others

Table 4. *Formal structure of 'Dialogue du vent et de la mer'*

Movement III		rondo/open	7:51	D♭	
1	first group		0:00		A
56	second group (always includes principal theme)	bar	1:20	C♯	B
80	first group		1:56		A
133	interlude with chorale	bar	3:14	D♭	C
157	second group	bar	4:10	D♭	B
195	climactic principal theme		5:26	>D♭	B
211	first group	rondo	5:54		A
244	second group with chorale	bar	6:41	D♭	B
270	synthesis of two groups		7:18	D♭	[A/B]

in the entire work; if such a simple interpretation is sustained, then the principal theme represents the sea (such a literal interpretation hardly does justice to Debussy's subtly allusive language). Whatever one chooses to call the first cyclic motif as it is employed here, it is of a leitmotivic character in a Wagnerian sense; its end is indeterminate as to cadence, it is capable of numerous transformations, and it falls outside the periodic phrase structure of the second group.

The principal theme of the second group ('the sea') is powerfully evocative of the Romantic second-subject style of the Russian symphonists and French counterparts; its phrase structure and association with the more conciliatory tones of the woodwind have a yearning character not met elsewhere in *La mer*. Dark undercurrents are present in the driving triplet string figures that rumble underneath at each presentation (except its central statement and 'Romantic' climax – bars 157–202; see Ex. 24a). A mediating motif spawned from the principal theme at bar 72 has a more neutral character; it can therefore occur in either thematic grouping. This is motif x, a core motif in *La mer* with variants in the first movement (see Ex. 14) and traces in the second; it proliferates in the third. In 'Dialogue du vent et de la mer' it is first heard in a raw form at III/25, then transposed into a lyrical form capable of maintaining the phraseology and flow of the principal theme (see Ex. 24b). Towards the end of the movement, it is translated into a generalised version of itself (and the principal theme), shorn of its characteristic rhythm and appoggiatura. Ex. 25 shows three stages in this development.

Ex. 24a/b   III/56–8, III/72–3

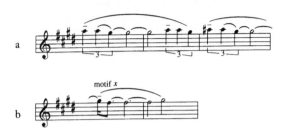

Ex. 25 III/45–6, 72–3, 258

III/80: first group

The regularity and relative predictability of the previous section seem to be lost as we return to the uncertainties of the first group. The harmony is constantly shifting and registral definition is volatile. Nevertheless, the repetition of bars 82–3 transposed up by a perfect fourth in bars 92–3 not only re-establishes regular periodicity, it also reveals Debussy to be using model-and-sequence construction to generate excitement in a manner far removed from the music of the first two movements.

The potential for regular patterning of the phrase structure enters a new phase at bar 94 when all harmonic movement is arrested. A treble ostinato figure, based on the ♪♪.♪ rhythm of the first movement's second principal section, accompanies a new derivative of motif x, thrillingly scored for unison horns, which alternates with a whole-tone version of the first cyclic motif. This is subject to model-and-sequence treatment as the music moves furiously towards a dynamic peak. The wave breaks in bar 118.

III/133: interlude with chorale

Rhetorical cause and effect may not enter *La mer* in the way checks and balances nourish logical discourse in a classical symphony, but Debussy's innovative acceptance of certain traditions means that one of the greatest dynamic peaks is followed by a passage of great calm. Muted trills in the divided cello accompany the return of the chorale that closed 'De l'aube à midi sur la mer'. The surface of the water here is gentle, the tranquillity complete.

III/157: second group

The bass moves from A♭ to D♭ in a way that cries out for conventional labelling – it is surely a perfect cadence. As the seesaw rocks once from a bass heavy A♭ to a treble-dominated D♭ harmony there is, however, little sense of a cadence, only the incorporation of the original A♭ into a full triad, which is not at all the same thing. Whatever one's reading of this passage, the return of the principal theme is initially a moment of peace and inwardness. Within a few bars, the propensity of the music to accelerate back to its original tempo after a drop in pulse, coupled with minute disturbances from tremolo strings, indicates that the peace is to be short-lived. After the principal theme is repeated, a major escalation in activity begins and the harmony departs from the static D♭ triad to pass across a tritone axis based primarily on C and F♯ (the tritone of the opening); this has the effect of a dominant and leads to one of *La mer*'s many revelations: the ecstatic reprise of the principal theme in the manner of a Romantic symphony or concerto.

III/195: climactic principal theme

All the vestiges of a traditional Romantic climax masquerade under this superlative piece of compositional design. The finale of Tchaikovsky's First Piano Concerto, like that of Sibelius's First Symphony, comes to the boil with a full-blooded restatement of the principal theme and then goes into cadential overdrive, all passion spent. At first appearances, this bold stroke of Debussy's is an uncharacteristic return to the nineteenth century; on closer inspection, however, it becomes clear that it is a deceptive climax rather like an interrupted cadence. It presages more integrated and characteristic climactic material that is still several bars away, and perpetuates the 'dialogue' between the states of the two motivic groups, bringing the principal theme fully into the lyrical domain, shorn of the driving elements hitherto associated with it; the accompanying voices are now just that – accompaniment.

III/211: first group

Driven by a new permutation of the quaver triplets that have provided so much of the dynamism in this movement, all the main motivic elements of the 'Dialogue du vent et de la mer' except the principal theme are sucked into a whirling vortex of activity, vividly conveyed by these lines of Poe: 'the vast bed of the waters seamed and scarred into a thousand conflicting channels, burst suddenly into frenzied convulsion – heaving, boiling, hissing – gyrating in gigantic and innumerable vortices'.[26] All this is grouped in regular phrase units of from two to five bars, building up a kinetic energy unprecedented in Debussy's music, driving towards the cumulative statement of the chorale in the next section. Motif x, the second limb of the principal theme, is also involved in this, as is the first cyclic motif, which now takes on some of the character of the principal theme itself. The transferral of characteristics from one thematic group to another, such a feature of this movement, reaches a new level in this section.

As elsewhere, the dynamic markings in the score are quieter than most performances would lead one to expect. Debussy's calculated effect is based upon a stratification of activity in which the components move at different speeds, all registering clearly by dint of the excellent balance that can be achieved when the score's dynamic values are observed. So the first cyclic motif at I/225 moves in crotchet duplets and triplets and minims whilst the busy textures beneath move in quaver triplets arranged in half-bar units. The 'conflicting channels' of the Poe story find a perfect musical analogue in this passage.

Shortly before the final return of the principal theme, its second limb is heard in stark isolation with the triplet figure suddenly silent (bar 237). This dramatic passage originally maintained the preceding quaver-triplet rhythm in the form of the famous, or infamous, fanfares on the second half of the first bar of each two-bar phrase, with the exception of the last (bars 243–4), where it is delayed and curtailed (the pause for breath before bar 245 added by some conductors here has no sanction in the score). Their excision changes the formal and expressive character of the passage.

III/244: second group with chorale

After the 'Romantic' statement of the principal theme at III/195, it now returns to its original state with driving triplets in several accompanying voices. However at III/258 the most startling transformation takes place as the principal theme is transmuted into an accompanying figure based on the quaver-triplet figuration; in rich, tolling sonorities beneath it, the chorale now rings resplendently through the texture.[27]

III/270: synthesis of two groups

The maelstrom of the closing moments of *La mer* is uniquely exciting. A series of powerful cadential plunges sends semiquavers, heard for the first time in the movement, plummeting through several octaves into the bass regions. Many motifs are sucked into this activity, including the first cyclic motif and the second limb (motif x) of the principal theme (see Ex. 24). From III/278 the first cyclic theme sets up a series of ostinatos in contradictory metres over which motif x pushes through in the heavy brass. The strongest cadential gesture in *La mer* occurs at III/283–6 when the bass moves from B♭ to G♮ to D♭, the G articulating a typical tritone cadence onto the tonic chord. Now, finally, we are 'home' and the various motivic elements simultaneously set up a triumphant peal which only stops with the *fff* wind trills at III/290.

7

Material and 'immaterial' music

Debussy spent much of his life in rebellion against the stylistic priorities of his contemporaries. Anything that confined the imagination, provided easy solutions, or smacked of contrivance was repugnant to one who proudly confided to his publisher in 1907 that *Rondes de printemps* (orchestral *Images*) was 'immaterial' music, not to be handled 'as though it were a robust symphony, walking on all four feet'.[1] 'Immateriality' may be less pronounced in *La mer*, *Rondes* being later, but *La mer*'s strong outline should not obscure its freedom from convention. A vital component of this freedom is *La mer*'s evolution of new processes to suit the changing environment of each movement and, indeed, each section. The form of the first movement gives a crude indication of how these evolving processes appear when described in schematic terms: 'ABCDE' may not denote a musical process, but as a means of organising material in a symphonic work it is stunningly original. Each section, moreover, evolves new means of articulation and expression. In harmonic terms, for example, the introduction and first principal section are largely based on the acoustic scale on D♭ (later on E); in contrast, the second principal section uses the Dorian mode on C (some would argue the major mode on B♭); the coda re-employs the acoustic scale on D♭ but omits its C♭. In short, each section has a different modal structure.

The succession of different chordal types used in 'Jeux de vagues' to characterise and demarcate the progressive changes from short-term to long-term rhythmic and motivic organisation is another example. At the opening, tense dissonances incorporating major sevenths are used, to be superseded in the sustained music of the second half by softer dissonances with minor sevenths, and finally a major triad (triads have almost no place in the first half of the movement). Few symphonic works of the nineteenth century exhibited such freedom. Even in *Tristan*, a progressive structure if ever there was one, the prelude encompasses almost the full harmonic range of the opera, including most of the four-note harmonies arising from the 'Tristan chord', and many primary motivic features are exposed there (or in the tenor monody that follows). It is a striking feature of *La mer* that the pentatonic figures and harmonies that open 'De l'aube à midi sur la mer' play almost no part in 'Jeux de vagues'; neither are the chromatic progressions of the finale's principal theme prefigured in 'De l'aube à midi sur la mer'. If one did not know *La mer*, one might believe that the three movements were separate works (in comparison with the differences enumerated, the return of the cyclic motifs is a minor matter).

The evolution of harmony, rhythm, and other parameters across the three movements results in what I have chosen to call 'narratives', all closely related. There is no evidence that Debussy's 'symphonic poem' tells a story, not even one as slight as Glazunov's work with the same title. But what *La mer* does have in common with a literary story is a sequence of musical events that echoes narrative devices such as an introductory paragraph or the speeding up of events as one reaches a climax. The ordering of these events is not accidental: what occurs at the opening of a movement is unlikely to be repeated later, but subsequent musical developments form part of a carefully-ordered progression from opening to closure. These narratives account for the deep-seated sense of unity many have admired in *La mer*.

Rhythm and 'rhythmicised time'[2]

Time passing is a fundamental subject of any piece of music. Without the shaping and manipulation of one's sense of time in transit, most or all Western art music would lose its underlying reason for being. No matter how crucial tonal or motivic development may be, the manipulation of pulse, metric groupings of that pulse, and the arrangement of metric groupings into phrases and groups of phrases result in distinctive structures that are as crucial to the workings of a Haydn symphony as they are to *The Rite of Spring*. Unfortunately, much analytical work tends to take this as read and concentrates instead on tonal or motivic working to such an extent that one may forget the rhythmic component altogether. Although this may be excusable in the study of Haydn (I am not convinced of this), the shaping of time in *La mer* has as much control over the structure as harmonic or motivic development – it cannot be overlooked. Rhythm is a premise in the narrative sense discussed above: its character evolves from section to section and from movement to movement in as notable a way as the motivic implications of the first bars of Brahms's Second Symphony continue to reverberate in the closing fanfares of the finale.

In an extra-musical sense, the narrative aspect of time passing is most explicit

76

Ex. 26   II/36–9, 163–6

in the title of the first movement, 'De l'aube à midi sur la mer', where there is a progression from one part of the day to another, vividly depicted in the diverse states of musical activity. Neither the second nor third movement title evokes a similar progression; yet at a musical level they develop and build on what is set out musically in the first movement.

To illustrate this, I begin with 'Jeux de vagues', whose function as a fulcrum between the outer movements makes it the most complex and rewarding movement to study in detail. The aspect of rhythm concentrated on is phrase structure.

A unique quality of this movement is the gradual transformation from a state of discontinuity in Parts 1 and 2, epitomised by a fragmented, edgy succession of events, to an expansive, continuous flow in Parts 3 and 4. Taking one of the few recapitulated passages as exemplar (Ex. 26), this can be sampled in the layout of dynamic, articulative, and accompanimental features. Notice the way articulation in bars 36–9 emphasises the individual bar at the expense of the four-bar unit, while in bars 163–6 the dynamics and accompanying figuration are continuous through the violin and cello parts.[3] This is a rare example of a motivic return that makes its point by variation; it is more usual in 'Jeux de vagues' to find new motivic material chosen that suits the different states of rhythmic development. In the first two parts motifs have a short-winded, interjectory character, while Part 3 has a single, long-breathed melody which is developed by sequence and other traditional methods within a recurring four-bar structure (II/171ff).

Ex. 27a/b   II/62–5, 171–4

The first eight bars of 'Jeux de vagues' establish a model for the rest of the movement, the final transformation of which results in the sustained melody of Part 3 and the resolving harmonic progressions of Part 4. The nature of this change is expressed below using eight-bar phrase structures, which are characteristic of the two halves:

$$\text{Parts 1 and 2: } 2 \pm 2 \ ! \ 2 \pm 2$$

$$\text{Parts 3 and 4: } 2 + 2 > 2 + 2$$

± passive continuation (or tangential continuation)
! deflection
+ active continuation
> leading to

'Passive continuation' occurs when the second phrase in a pair ('unit') fails to react to the implications of the first. Repetition without development is a prime example of this, for it is static – a denial of the first phrase's existence. Tangential continuation is less extreme, involving a voice-leading break or change of harmony that undermines continuity from the first phrase to the second (many degrees of relationship are meant by the term 'passive continuation'). In both examples, emphasis is upon beginning afresh, though motivic material is often shared. 'Active continuation' is the opposite state, whose most highly developed form would be an antecedent–consequent unit. Ex. 27 shows instances of tangential and active continuation.

Ex. 28   II/1–2, 5–6, 7–8

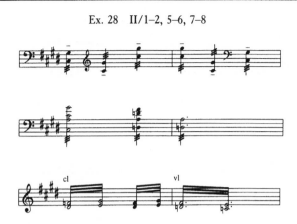

In bars 1–8 Debussy defines the temporal space, laying down parameters to be extended and moulded. The basic element is the two-bar phrase, defined in bars 1–2 by a sustained wind chord and string tremolo figure. This phrase is to be the common denominator throughout the movement, for subsequent phrases derive from it; always by duration, and sometimes by absorbing features like the tremolo strings and sustained wind chords, both of which reverberate through the dissolving musical fabric of bars 5–8. Thus bars 1–2 function like a rhythmic *ground* in a passacaglia, reinforced by these other features (see Ex. 28).

The static repetition of bars 1–2 is the first example of passive continuation. That the music is now to proceed by a series of disruptions is immediately apparent, for in bar 4 the flutes cut across the second two-bar phrase, anticipating bars 5–8, which are to break down the modest level of continuity experienced so far (the subject of stratification in *La mer* caused by features such as the flute's entry, which seems to create a secondary phrase structure, is an absorbing one).

Part 2 (bar 36) opens with a template of the climactic material of Part 3 (bar 163) with two-bar phrases tentatively bonding into pairs. Two four-bar units resemble a sentence structure, namely, statement and counterstatement.[4] In the third unit, the developmental part of a sentence, the two-bar *ground*, previously submerged, regains its primacy as passive continuation begins to take over again. The manner in which this happens is related to the opening bars of the movement by tremolando figures that reappear at this point in the violas. After these twelve bars, the flow is interrupted: the two-bar cello B in bars 48–9 alone holds onto a fragment of the foregoing. Two harps 'wash' the

Debussy: *La mer*

Ex. 29   II/97–103

sudden vacuum with their glissandos, offering a new variation on the *ground* and reinstating the rhythmic model of bars 1–8.

A new stage in the process is reached when the first recapitulation passes almost imperceptibly across the bow, still in Part 2. A new phrase group appears that can be represented $2 \pm 1 \pm 2$ (bars 92–6). This may seem a dubious way to promote the growth of a bonded four-bar unit, but its function becomes obvious when its five-bar organisation is immediately taken up in the next, freshly-minted phrase group, and reinforced. This beautiful passage (bars 97–103) has the rhythmic organisation $2 > 1 > 2 \pm 2$. The 'orphan' bar (99) attempts to establish active continuation between the two-bar phrases on either side of it; the use of a crescendo across the orphan bar and the shape of the motif are two of several attributes that give it a connecting or leading character. Thus the passage represents an interim stage in the drive to active continuation in bonded units (see Ex. 29).

In Part 3 bonded four-bar units initially produce statement–counterstatement (bars 163–70) just as they did in Part 2 (bars 36–43), but in place of the developmental unit and harp deflection heard in Part 2 at bar 48, we are now introduced to a glowing melody that borrows the leading one-bar figure of bar 99 (*x*), incorporating it twice into the first of two two-bar phrases, to produce a $2 + 2$ unit (see Ex. 27b). Leading between phrases to produce this bonded unit is ensured by the contour of *x*, which is strongly directed to the E of bar 173. The D♮ that concludes the unit moves semitonally to D♯, producing a voice-leading connection between bars 174 and 175 that can be represented $2 + 2 > 2 + 2$ (bars 171–8). This is pretty well the final transformation of the eight-bar model of the opening from a disjunct to a conjunct phrase group based on bonded units of four bars each. We now have the best conditions so far for sustained melody in *La mer*.

In a motivic sense the coda is a throwback to the two-bar tyranny of the first part of 'Jeux de vagues', but four-bar continuity has now passed to the harmonic domain, expressed through a series of voice-leading motions aimed at establishing the E major triad. These harmonic events mainly take place at four-bar intervals (with interpolated two-bar phrases), with the motivic

Ex. 30   II/219–28

elements in between subservient to them. The slow progress of the bass line from bar 219 demonstrates this (see Ex. 30).

The establishment of regular rhythmic structures in 'Jeux de vagues' participates in a broader process across the three movements. In 'De l'aube à midi sur la mer' we find variable phrase lengths and blurred boundaries, without the fragmentation and disruption of 'Jeux de vagues'; the rhythmic structure is very much at the mercy of this movement's diverse musical states. A consequence of this is the absence of statement–counterstatement or antecedent–consequent phrase groups. 'Jeux de vagues', on the other hand, immediately sets up a consistent phrase length from which to construct the regularity of Part 3, and introduces tentative statement–counterstatement groups.

From early on in 'Dialogue du vent et de la mer', motivic events themselves are responsible for the adoption of a regular periodic structure, usually based upon two- or four-bar phrases. This is impressed upon us by the partial symmetry of the principal theme, which takes the form $2 + 2 > 2 + 3$. Moreover, the second unit, a grouping of five bars, is a consequent: antecedent–consequent groups are common.

The motifs of the finale are fragmented in the closing stages, not in the sense of the opening of 'Jeux de vagues', but rather in the manner of a synthesis of diverse elements all consumed in the terrifying exultation of the grand-slam conclusion. These motivic fragments are subordinate to a now overwhelming

Ex. 31   III/266–77

organisation of harmonic and other parameters into connected four-bar units or phrases (see Ex. 31). Debussy has worked his way from a radical openness in the first half of *La mer* to a highly individual assimilation in the finale of the question-and-answer phraseology of the nineteenth-century work. 'Immateriality' secedes to 'materiality'.

Motif and arabesque

One cannot rewrite the history of music analysis in the hope that the age-old obsession with motivic unity (based on development) might somehow be rectified. Schoenberg, Reti, Epstein, and others too numerous to list have made the investigation of motivic unity the linchpin of their work, especially where symphonic music or music involving the sonata principle is involved. Schenker is one of very few major analytical theorists to run counter to this – his concept of motif is distinctive – but his methods were not intended to be of use in the discussion of Debussy.

La mer tends not to depend upon motivic unification and development in the Brahms or d'Indy mould for coherence. Indeed, the composer himself expressed varying degrees of nausea when confronted by development sections. Emile Vuillermoz recalled Debussy's description of his escape 'the previous evening from a concert where a Beethoven quartet was being played, just at the moment when the "old deaf one" started to "develop a theme"'.[5] In *La mer* there is as much a quest for motivic diversity as for motivic homogeneity. As the sea's changing states are explored, new motivic shapes evolve, some incorporating elements from existing ones, many others freshly minted for the moment at hand. In the introduction to 'De l'aube à midi sur la mer' motivic disparity is set up as a premise from which the movement proceeds with a consistency that is not seriously challenged by the cellular relationship between certain motifs. Ex. 32 shows the four motifs of the introduction and highlights the differences in timbre, rhythm, length, and affective character, whilst recognising the shared three-note cell.

Disparity gives way to a passage of sustained motivic development in Part 3 of 'Jeux de vagues' that unites disparate features from earlier in the movement. The motif-driven finale then progresses towards a growing degree of motivic unanimity. The closing bars of the work throw various motivic threads into the melting pot, obliterating their most distinctive features. By this stage Debussy has moved as far away as possible from the conditions prevailing in the first movement's introduction. All of which is evidence enough that there

Ex. 32   I/3–5, 6–9, 8, 12–13

is a melodic narrative running through *La mer* comparable to other parameters.

Debussy's rejection of symphonic development as it was understood by his contemporaries is reflected in the way the two cyclic motifs remain aloof from the motivic action around them, rather than determining it. Barraqué uses the term *thème objectif* to define this downgrading of the cyclic motifs so that they become a product of the motivic discourse rather than its subject.[6] Whereas Gilson's *La mer* portentously declares its cyclic motif at the beginning and then triumphantly repeats it at the end, Debussy makes only a veiled use of his first cyclic motif in 'De l'aube à midi sur la mer'. In the introduction (I/9) it steals in, cutting across the descending violin tremolo in a manner characteristic of the blurred phrase outlines of the movement. As the central point in the introduction's arch form (abcba), it is unrepeated, yielding precedence to motif *x* and the ascending arpeggiations of bars 3–5. The first cyclic motif does not recur until the first principal section is in decay, and it once again overlaps with another motif. It is accorded the same treatment at the end of the second principal section, sneaking in unobtrusively as whole-tone harmonies replace the previously clear tonal definition of the cello theme. On each occasion, its shape and character are unlike the motivic features on which it intrudes, so its effect is of a motivic 'dissonance'.

The first cyclic motif's status changes dramatically in 'Dialogue du vent et de la mer', where it is a dynamic musical participant in the first group. By the end of the movement the entire contrapuntal fabric is saturated with it, and in the process it loses its leitmotivic open-endedness in terms of phrase length, becoming part of the increasingly regular periodic structure (a point vividly illustrated in bars 98ff).

Ex. 33   I/32–4

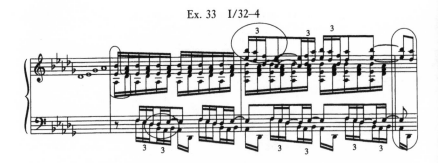

The manner in which events unfold from bar to bar is infinitely fascinating, for one experiences time after time the sensation that an idea is familiar, even when its surface bespeaks disparity and incongruity. Barraqué was much struck by this phenomenon, and the following examples draw to some extent on his work. Ex. 33 demonstrates how the intervallic material of much of the introduction and first principal section of 'De l'aube à midi sur la mer' is based on the intervals of a pair of major seconds separated by a minor third, or three-note subsets of that (e.g. E♭–D♭–B♭); this operates as an unordered set in that its ordering may vary and the pairs of seconds rotate to produce a perfect fourth's separation between them. This makes it cellular along the lines described by Schoenberg in his brief analytical sketches of works such as Beethoven's String Quartet in F minor, Op. 95 (*Quartetto serioso*) and Brahms' Fourth Symphony. The cell inhabits melodic and harmonic domains at the opening, the overlapping entries of the basses and harps producing the sonority B–F♯–G♯, to which C♯ is finally added in bar 3. It rubs off on the first cyclic motif, but it is not until the beginning of the first principal section that the rich use to which such an idea can be put is revealed. In Ex. 33 the four-note figure invades accompaniment and harmony. It is in every sense pervasive, contributing to the blurred tonal definition of the section by burying the D♭ major triad. The cell's influence extends to the second principal section as well, though its three-note subset is most in evidence, as the opening B♭–C–G figure makes plain.

Two motivic constellations exist in *La mer*. The first includes the principal theme of 'Dialogue du vent et de la mer' and the two cyclic motifs, which are concentrated, polished motivic gestures rather like Wagner's leitmotifs in their immediate recognisability and power of suggestion; they would not be out of place in one of the many Franco-Wagnerian operas of the period. The other constellation comprises motifs whose character is more diffuse: they are malleable in rhythmic terms, capable of undergoing many metamorphoses,

Ex. 34   motif and arabesque: II/44, 171–2

bar 44

bars 171–2

and liable to end up in the delicate tracery of motivically insignificant arabesque.

Bars 6ff of 'De l'aube à midi sur la mer' bear the most significant of these motifs, motif *x*. It is encountered in various forms throughout the first movement, and yields several derivations in the 'Dialogue du vent et de la mer'. It crystallises into a fully 'finished' motif only when certain of its characteristics are subsumed into the Franckian principal theme.

Some of Debussy's most famous declarations of musical allegiance were to the 'divine arabesque' of Palestrina, Lassus, and Bach. André Fontainas recalled one of Debussy's many statements of artistic intent that is closely related to the Renaissance and Baroque music Debussy so admired for its use of arabesque. He is reported to have said that he would find 'a music truly free of motifs, or formed of one continuous motif that nothing interrupts and will never go back over itself. So it will develop logically, tightly, deductively.'[7] Anyone seeking a practical realisation of this will surely be struck by the way many of Debussy's motifs fail to continue in a rhetorical manner, trailing off instead into continuous, flowing lines that are insignificant in terms of intervallic or rhythmic definition. Françoise Gervais draws analogies with art and architecture when he writes of some decorative art as '*ornamental* and *not figurative*'.[8]

Fully-fledged motifs such as the cyclic motifs and principal theme of the finale have an emblematic character that seems the opposite of the flowing melodic type Debussy evokes in his idealised statement. These motifs are subject to development and recapitulation, making their contrast with other motifs a subject for discourse. Some of the unformulated or unfinished motifs, however, do correspond to our understanding of musical arabesque; their employment alongside explicitly finished motifs suggests that arabesque was just one of several resources Debussy used in *La mer*, not an end in itself. Part of this resource involves the transformation of arabesque into motif, most conspicuously seen in the evolution of the sustained melody of 'Jeux de vagues' from arabesque-like figures in bar 44 (see Ex. 34). The manner of its derivation does not cry out for recognition: it is not the obvious metamorphosis of a motif characteristic of Liszt and Wagner, but rather a background feature that emerges from arabesque to reveal itself as motif, a trivial growth in some ways that still manages to produce a satisfying level of integration while avoiding any sense of rhetorical development.

Tonality

Tonality is one of the main narratives in *La mer*. Its force is felt in the development of different harmonic types to characterise each section, and in the linking of sections by prominent treble pitches which contribute to a process of tonic definition that gathers force as the work proceeds. These treble pitches are close enough to Schenkerian concepts such as 'primary melodic tone' and 'fundamental line' to warrant a brief discussion of voice leading in *La mer* before going on to examine their structural role. Voice leading involves the connection of voices, the inner voices as well as treble and bass, according to principles loosely derived from strict counterpoint. Such progressions scarcely exist in *La mer*; harmonies are not connected to each other in this way except in rare passages such as the coda of 'Jeux de vagues', where voice leading serves a strictly localised purpose. There is nevertheless a coincidence with Schenkerian theory. From early on in the first movement we find a treble emphasis on B♭. One may hear this in bars 31ff, where it is first heard oscillating against A♭, and then carried up into its usual register in bar 33. It has an ambiguous appoggiatura character here, but a few bars later, in bar 43, the status of B♭ crystallises in the new motif of the oboe, harp, and solo viola, which is immediately reinforced by a static B♭ in the first violins. From this point, there is a dialectic between B♭, as a kind of anti-tonic, and A♭ as the privileged representative of the tonic triad ('tonic triad' is more an aspiration than a reality at this stage – it only gathers force in the last movement). B♭ and A♭/G♯ are 'prolonged' as focal pitches by upper and lower auxiliaries. In I/51 B♮ takes over for eight bars before the poignant oboe motif leads us back to B♭. Various gestures hint at the ultimate primacy of the D♭ major triad with A♭ on top, not least the final cadence of 'De l'aube à midi sur la mer' in which B♭ overlaps with a D♭ major triad sustained in the middle register.

In 'Jeux de vagues' the opening chord picks up A♭, as G♯, of the D♭ major chord that ended 'De l'aube à midi sur la mer'. The pitch continues to reverberate through the movement until its place is taken by B♭, dramatically repeated by harps as we move towards the movement's climax. In making extensive use of a tritone 'dominant' in 'Jeux de vagues', Debussy keeps active the A♭–B♭ conflict in a less concentrated manner. As the title of this movement implies, tonality is in 'play' here; in the third movement it is to be drastically consolidated.

In III/9 the treble line is reactivated with the oboe's G♯. This pitch is to be repeatedly articulated in the principal theme (from bar 56). Notice the way the lead up to this, and the principal theme itself, make use of a number of treble progressions down from A, B♭, or B to the G♯. This is the third and final phase in the narrative. The first involved B♭ as the primary treble pitch that rendered the D♭ major triad ambiguous in 'De l'aube à midi sur la mer'. The second threw the two elements into 'play' by making B♭ the main dominant in 'Jeux de vagues'. And the third makes G♯/A♭ the focal pitch of the main motifs of 'Dialogue du vent et de la mer', so preparing the way for the final chord which, inevitably, has A♭ uppermost and transforms B♭ into an ornamental appoggiatura to it.

Keys, modes, and modulations

A conventional reading of tonality in *La mer* leads seductively to key schemes for the three movements along these lines:

Movement I: B minor (bar 1), D♭ major (bar 31), E major (from around bar 52 or later), B♭ major (bar 84), D♭ major (bar 122)

Movement II: E major (F♭ major)

Movement III: C♯ minor/D♭ major

Inevitably, such a scheme has to accommodate the many deviations from these areas, such as a move towards A-based harmonies in the second movement, but its general appositeness would not be open to question. As an overview of the three movements it offers a typical key arrangement for a symphonic work in the classical manner, there being many nineteenth-century examples of the flat mediant's use for the central movement. Following various nineteenth-century precedents, it might also be pointed out that Debussy softens the move from E major of the second movement by going first to C♯ minor in the finale before arriving at D♭ major in the central portion of the movement.

That the harmonic organisation of *La mer* is centripetal cannot be denied. Each movement may be satisfactorily explained in terms of a tonic of some sort, usually associated, at least in the closing bars, with a major triad. But if one moves a little closer to the substance of the music – its real sound and notation – one soon realises that major-minor tonality has very little to do with

Ex. 35   Main pitch collections in introduction to first movement
(accompanying voices shown as filled note heads)

bars 1–5

bars 6–9

bars 9–17

the tonal materials of *La mer*. The opening of the first movement, the slow
introduction, centres on a bass B in bar 1, which is subsequently taken up in
the highest voice as the violins make their slow descent from bar 6. So B is
the focal pitch, and, as it happens, the key signature is two sharps, which
promises B minor. If this were indeed B minor one would expect more than
a focal pitch and key signature, however; one would seek a cadence of some
sort onto a B minor triad, usually supported by at least the leading note A♯.
In fact, neither a leading note nor a cadence can be found in the introduction,
though a trace of the triad can be heard in the bass progression from B in
bar 5 to D in bar 17. This opens out a major sixth – a component of the tonic
triad. The B minor triad is otherwise absent, and A♯ is nowhere to be heard;
rather, the oboe makes considerable play on an A♮ in bars 6–9.

Thus the evidence is overwhelmingly against accepting B minor as a useful
denominator for the slow introduction. It is more helpful to investigate the
pitch collections Debussy actually uses. These are all modes of various types,
usually with a flat seventh (as in the Dorian mode), and often with a raised
fourth (as in the acoustic scale). Debussy's use of modes is very free, especially
in the manner in which the tonic pitch is allowed to float.[9] Ex. 35 shows the
main pitch collections used in the slow introduction. In keeping with the
motivic and rhythmic structure of this section, it is worth noting the way in
which different pitch collections overlap and intersect as, for example, when
the first cyclic motif is adumbrated in bars 9–11.

The opening of the *modéré* seems to offer clearer linear triadic definition than we have heard at any point in the introduction; the harps and violas both play A♭ and D♭, while the divided cellos arpeggiate the full major triad, albeit with a prominent B♭ separating F from A♭. In spite of this, one does not hear the D♭ triad by itself, for throughout this passage the pitches E♭ and B♭ are heard at the beginning of each quaver in the second violins; these pitches are then incorporated into the pentatonic motif first heard in bar 33 (Ex. 16) in the flutes and clarinets. The first four bars of the *modéré* contain five notes, all of which belong to the D♭ major scale, lacking only the fourth and seventh pitches (G♭ and C) to complete it. When we finally hear a seven-note scale upon the entry of the horn motif in bar 35, it is not a major one but a mode based on a raised fourth and lowered seventh (D♭–E♭–F–G–A♭–B♭–C♭). Comparison with the first cyclic motif reveals a similar intervallic construction. Given the prevalence of the cyclic motif in the first and third movements, it is easy to see why much of the harmonic organisation is based on this mode.

The weakness of the argument that upholds the major mode as a constituent becomes even more apparent when one considers the first passage in the work, where the acoustic scale gives way to what appears to be a diatonic major one; this occurs in the second principal section with the celebrated cello theme in bar 84. Once again Debussy offers us what appears to be an unambiguous key signature, namely B♭ major, but the triad of that key plays only a modest part in this passage. In the melodic cadences it is C rather than B♭ that is emphasised; there is no cadential emphasis on B♭ (though one does hear that pitch with its major triad at the beginning of bar 87). The focus on C is reinforced a few bars later when, at the apex of the *en animant* development of the cello theme, the harmony suddenly lands on a C major triad in bar 95. Given the shortage of moments of such harmonic clarity, one should not undervalue the light they shed on the tonal organisation. The use of a B♭ scale with emphasis on C points to a strongly Dorian inflection in this passage.

Dogmatism about this issue would hardly benefit our understanding of *La mer*. Ambiguity is a feature of the first movement and, to a lesser extent, of the second as well. Part of this ambiguity lies in the contest between adjacent pitches for emphasis, a feature that is well demonstrated by the bass in bar 105, where it is not clear whether the focus is on B♭ or C, and at the end of the movement, where the woodwind cadences on B♭ but the brass insists on a D♭ triad, producing a certain ambivalence as to the tonal allegiance of the movement (the D♭ triad lasts longest).

As in a major or minor key work, there is modulation. This functions in much the same way as in a traditional context, except that there are three basic modes in 'De l'aube à midi sur la mer': the acoustic, the Dorian, and the whole-

Ex. 36   change to mode based on E in I/57–62

tone scale, which comes into operation at the close of the second principal section and colours the interlude. The modes are subject to transposition and alteration, just as they would be in a D♭ major work. As the first principal section enters its final phase it is clear that the scale based on D♭ has been supplanted by the same on E (anticipating the tonic of 'Jeux de vagues'). This functions melodically in the form of the cyclic theme, in the bass progression which picks out pitches of the scale, and harmonically. The integration of the motivic, bass, and harmonic domains is strongly reminiscent of triadic tonal music as viewed by Schenkerian theory, as is the importance given to treble pitches at various points in the movement (discussed above). Ex. 36 shows a passage where the scale based on E is gradually assuming control of these domains.

In comparison with the first movement, the second is more chromatic in pitch content, and also more strongly hierarchic in its harmonic organisation. Nevertheless, the acoustic scale's raised fourth (A♯) is present and attached to various tonics, especially E, but there is often a raised leading note (D♯) – a feature almost unique to this movement. E major is present only in the closing bars in the form of a triad – never as a scale. Whole-tone scales also make their presence felt.

Modally, the third movement has two underlying characteristics. The first of these is determined by the first cyclic motif that brings with it the acoustic scale. In dialogue with this is the principal theme, first heard with a C♯ minor triad. In a certain sense, this is the most traditional element in *La mer*, a motif that flourishes in a self-propagating manner within two- or three-bar phrases. When it is heard in the first half of the movement, it is supported by minor harmonies, and major harmonies in the second half; yet a review of its total pitch content indicates a highly chromatic organisation with a 'Phrygian' second step (D♮). So even here, Debussy is still at some remove from major/ minor tonality. As the movement reaches its ecstatic close, the acoustic scale re-establishes itself without the flat seventh (there is neither a C nor a C♭ in the closing bars of *La mer*), confirming this scale as the primary method of organisation, and relating the close of this movement to that of the first.

Harmony

Debussy made his feelings on the subject of Conservatoire-style harmony well known in his writings and letters, and in the famous conversations with Ernest Guiraud.[10] In a characteristically forthright article he wrote, 'The best thing one could wish for French music would be to see the study of harmony abolished as it is practised in our conservatories. It is the most ridiculous way of arranging notes.'[11]

La mer breaks with the harmonic language of its predecessors. The old hierarchy founded on tonic, subdominant, and dominant supported by a series of root progressions hardly exists, and is rarely encountered in his other music.[12] Many chords are based on four or five notes, and look like dominant sevenths or ninths but without leading to, or even implying, a tonic triad. This is not to say that there is no sense of hierarchy or function in *La mer*'s harmonies, only that they are devised in a style that is either unique to its context or to this stage in the composer's career.

'Harmonic syntax' means recurring harmonies with, above all, cadential function. Integration in a Bach chorale is secured by tonal progressions which, in the course of a phrase, run through various harmonies beginning with a primary or secondary tonic, followed by some form of supertonic or subdominant (or submediant or weakened form of the tonic), which precedes a dominant harmony rhythmically placed as an upbeat to a tonic downbeat. Most of these phrases use triads or sevenths based on the degrees of a major or minor scale. 'Dominant' usually denotes the harmony rooted on the fifth degree of the major or minor scale. This practice informed most tonal music up to the end of the nineteenth century, though the syntax became freer, especially in Wagner.

Debussy broke with tradition in a profounder, more disruptive way than Wagner, without straying into the lonely atonal territory soon to be explored by Schoenberg and his pupils. One looks in vain for progressions founded on archetypes. As has already been demonstrated, none of the movements makes use of a major or minor scale: the acoustic scale, the commonest mode, lacks

Ex. 37   harmonic progression from introduction to first principal section, I/30–1

a crucial component of the old harmonic system, namely the raised seventh or leading note (C natural in D♭ major). Perfect cadences containing a move from a dominant triad or seventh to a tonic triad are the exception not the rule in *La mer* (one each in the second and third movements).

Harmonies often progress without one being weighted in such a way that it yields to another in a cadential manner. This lack of clear-cut cadences is most apparent in 'De l'aube à midi sur la mer', where there are many fresh starts as new material or sections get underway, though few of them are launched harmonically by a cadence from a previous section. One would expect the transition from the slow introduction to the *modéré* to use harmonic as well as rhythmic and textural means to link the sections. As it transpires, the launch of the new section is weak harmonically, showing few residual characteristics of a dominant-tonic progression (see Ex. 37). The upbeat chord contains both the root and the fifth of D♭ and offers no direct semitone transfer to aid continuity. Moreover, the two chords are so differently characterised orchestrally and registrally that there is little sense of harmonic connection.

There are also few moments where the music is disposed to rest in a 'falling' or cadential manner: when it does, cadential articulation is as much motivic as harmonic. So the two principal types of harmonic cadence, those that link one phrase or section to the next, and those that bring local closure to a phrase or section, are rarities. These rarities evolve their own syntax, which is the subject of the next few paragraphs.

'Jeux de vagues' mediates between the harmonic informality of the first movement and the triadic starting-point of the principal theme in the finale. Earlier parts of the movement indicate the presence of a tonic by substituting complex harmonies for the triad. At first these substitutions seem to bear little relationship to the tonic triad. The opening, for example, later proves to be an adumbration of the tonic, but at first one can only hazard a guess as to its position within the hierarchy. Later, after some strongly upbeat activity, we settle down into a passage of such assured regularity and clarity that we

Ex. 38   evolving versions of the tonic harmony in 'Jeux de vagues'

immediately pin our hopes of tonal resolution on it; this is a seventh founded on E. As the passage progresses Debussy produces more substitutions for the tonic before whole-tone harmonies take over. This is a cumulative, end-directed process, which begins with a vague idea of a tonic and ends with clearcut cadences onto a tonic triad derived from a series of prototypes (see Ex. 38).[13]

The 'dominant' that functions against the tonic in 'Jeux de vagues' is not founded on B♮ until the coda; it is usually called a 'dominant major ninth on B♭'. We first hear it in bar 28 when it is placed in a potentially upbeat relationship to the E⁷ harmony of bar 36 (Part 2). It returns prior to the A-based section of 92, where E is replaced as tonic. Its status is confirmed when it prepares the return of the material of bars 36ff at the beginning of Part 3 and erupts loudly at the climax of the same part in bar 211, having made its presence felt some bars before. The 'dominant' harmony pervades the coda until its position is usurped by an altered dominant on B♮.

Voice-leading progressions between the two harmonies – the tritone dominant and the tonic – occur only in the coda, where Debussy, as an additional compositional resource, starts to join up harmonies melodically. Here we find the tritone dominant yielding by chromatic steps to the tonic, which, at this stage, is still represented by the seventh harmony, though this is beginning to resolve via C♯ to a triad (see Ex. 39). The B♭ harmony is finally replaced by a dominant B♮ in the bar 237. A new motif mediates between new and old, picking up the major third A♭–C in the dominant ninth on B♭ and bringing it to A–C♯ of the new dominant. The motif's role is therefore to act as a go-between, effecting a transition from one dominant to another. This change recalls the way in which the first passage of tonal definition tailed off with what was, at the time, a weak continuation on B (bars 48ff), not the B♭ dominant, so making the final outcome a resumption and completion of unfinished business. Debussy's adoption of a new dominant does not bring with it a resolution of the leading note, or, for that matter, other dissonant

Ex. 39   II/233–45

Ex. 40   III/190–5

components of the altered dominant sonority (which contains all the pitches of the whole-tone scale on C♯), though as Ex. 39 shows, there are melodic links between the two harmonies.

In 'Dialogue du vent et de la mer' Debussy creates a sense of dominant–tonic function through a juxtaposition of oft-affirmed triadic statements of C♯/D♭ with ambiguous harmonic or melodic elements based on the tritone, usually the C–F♯ that figured so prominently in the previous movements. This deprives the music of any single harmonic element that could be called a dominant (in contrast to 'Jeux de vagues'), replacing it with a range of harmonies. One example will suffice to illustrate this. In the central part of the finale there is a long subdued passage over a D♭ pedal. At bar 179 this is replaced by fluctuating harmonies and a rapid build-up to the work's Romantic climax at bar 195. Ex. 40 shows how harmonies and melodic figures based on the tritone underscore the lead-up to the return of D♭ major, thereby simulating a dominant–tonic cadential progression. Elsewhere, in bars 63–4, a tritone dominant based on G leads to the repetition of the principal theme with tonic triad. This recalls the tritone dominant of 'Jeux de vagues' and creates a syntactical precedent for the final cadence of the work, which also uses the tritone.

The so-called 'perfect cadence' from bars 133–57 could be regarded as a

Ex. 41   Cadential progressions at I/137–41, II/131–63, III/278–92

nostalgic look back at nineteenth-century harmonic practice, but in addition to the objections to this view voiced in chapter 6 (see p. 72), there is also a prominent tritone polarity around A♭–D♮ that seems to take priority here, acting in a manner analogous to C–F♯ in bars 179–94.

The 'Dialogue' develops more active cadential progressions in its closing stages. A bass progression on an inversion of the three-note treble motif that closed 'De l'aube à midi sur la mer' (E♭–D♭–B♭) is a cadential determinant in bars 265–70, a passage that culminates in an explosive D♭ major chord. The bass moves A♭–B♭–(E♭)–B♭–D♭ and supports a weak harmonic progression of V–VI–I. The motivic progression's strength partly moves cadential activity out of the harmonic domain, just as it did in the first movement; this is not unexpected given the modal nature of the pitch organisation. The final cadence, however, reinstates harmonic articulation as the bass B♭–G♮–(A♭)–D♭ underpins strong harmonies. The dominant seventh on this G is a characteristic tritone dominant; it re-establishes a sense of normality in the harmonic world of *La mer*, leaving any hint of an orthodox 'perfect cadence' in the central episode (bars 133–57) a one-off aberration (like the Romantic climax that follows) in a work where such diversity is fundamental. This final cadence has its precedent in the concluding bars of 'De l'aube à midi sur la mer', when the cell E♭–D♭–B♭, mentioned above, is complemented by a B♭–D♭ bass progression;[14] and also in the build-up to, and beginning of, Part 3 of 'Jeux de vagues' (II/131–63), where the principal bass progression is G–B♭–E. However, a definitive cadential progression that draws together these precedents is heard only once: in the closing bars of *La mer*. That it is a logical, congruent event is assured by the adumbrations of it and the dismissal of traditional harmonic procedure from the first moments of the work (see Ex. 41).

8

Afterword

Debussy found his first orchestral work after *Pelléas* capable of rebutting both the favourable and unfavourable questions raised by critics and his own artistic conscience, but Laloy was surely wrong in his assessment of *La mer* as marking the beginning of a new phase in Debussy's development. In fact the major work he began directly after *La mer*'s composition (the orchestral *Images*) is strikingly free of the symphonic outline Laloy had remarked upon so forcefully; only in the final phase of his career did Debussy approach the symphonic style again, this time in chamber music. Many would also consider *La mer* unique among Debussy's works in the depth of feeling it reveals, especially in its final movement.

La mer was the last thing the loyal *Pelléastres* expected: even at the level of programme music and general manner Debussy confounded them by overtly depriving the work of many of the Impressionist attributes they had come to expect; and he added the subtitle 'symphonic sketches' lest there be any doubt about his intentions. He manipulated his reception in this way, drawn by both the instinctive and the calculating aspects of his creativity. If this makes him sound overly reactive to others' views, then a degree of calculation in the type of work he undertook should be considered alongside his intense reluctance to repeat himself from work to work, which had become something of an obsession with him, and was constantly demonstrated during the prolific period of *La mer*.

In a compositional sense, he turned *La mer* into a many-stranded étude in compositional technique by which he charted the relationship between past, present, and future in a way that scarcely any other twentieth-century work has attempted to do. This implies a narrative across the work variously described in this handbook as concerned with the passage of time, the evolution of phrase structures, increasingly 'solid' triadic definition, and so on. In each parameter, the time travelled is from the present to the past, assimilating with increasing sureness of touch those elements of musical language usually referred to as symphonic, most impressively displayed in the gestural behaviour of the last movement. This narrative applies equally to the role of repetition. In his writings and letters, one encounters diatribes against recapitulation – almost as many as against development; nevertheless, from a first movement that turns repetition into an elevated form of dissonance (the first cyclic motif), he uses modest levels of recapitulation in the second for structural turning points, and finally in 'Dialogue du vent et de la mer' he drives the movement to its extraordinary conclusion by three full repetitions of the principal theme, and then full-bloodedly restates the chorale motif of the first movement's coda. Like Wagner's *Meistersinger*, in which a deliberate link with a remote past is cast in thoroughly modern musical garb, *La mer* looks forwards and backwards, confounding critics and challenging preconceptions about musical style by successfully combining within one work 'immateriality' (Eimert's 'vegetative circulation of form') and 'materiality' in the form of a crisp symphonic outline.

This does not mean that *La mer* was Debussy's one experiment with the language of the Franckian symphony – his opportunity to rediscover the 'robust forms' he had rejected in successive works since the String Quartet. *La mer*'s symphonic mastery lies at a deeper level than the motivic developments and harmonic orthodoxies of the symphonic styles that surrounded him at the Société Nationale. It should have ensured that Debussy would forever be uncategorisable, but bad habits die hard; nevertheless, the challenge is there for those willing and able to rise to it.

La mer no longer suffers neglect in concert programmes or recording schedules. If the CD catalogue is a reliable guide to a work's popularity, then the forty or more versions now listed in the UK catalogue put it into the same league as Beethoven's Fifth. However, few, if any, of these recorded performances are an accurate representation of the score, or of Debussy's intentions expressed elsewhere; so we can have only an imprecise aural experience of *La mer*. This is partly bound up with the promiscuous approach engendered by *La mer*'s alleged Impressionism. Now, with a new edition and greater knowledge than ever before of how precise Debussy wished performances of his music to be, we may aspire to, if not expect, critical and interpretative rediscoveries of a well-concealed masterpiece that is as true to the French genius as the operas of Rameau so well loved by its author.

Notes

1 Debussy: 1903–1905

1 The questionnaire is repoduced in Dietschy, *A Portrait*, pp. 56–7.
2 'Debussy at sea', p. 641. The original account may be found in René Peter, *Claude Debussy, vues prises de son intimé* (Paris, 1944), pp. 112–25.
3 Dietschy, *A Portrait*, p. 138. An arrangement of another water piece, Schumann's piano duet 'Am Springbrunnen', Op. 85 as 'A la fontaine' for piano solo, is often attributed to 1904, when it was published by Fromont. In fact it first appeared in the musical supplement of *L'illustration* (September 1895), pp. 148–52.
4 In Rolf, 'Debussy's *La mer*', pp. 1–2.
5 The hitherto unknown extent of Debussy's involvement with the Société Nationale has been examined by Teresa Davidian, whose paper 'Debussy, d'Indy and the *Société Nationale*' was given at the *Journées Claude Debussy*, Institut Français, London, 30 September 1993. A rather different Debussy emerged in this paper that contrasts with the rebellious one so often portrayed in biographies.
6 *Letters*, p. 136.
7 Dietschy, *A Portrait*, p. 129. This is the most revealing biography for Debussy's psychological motivation, but Dietschy's unsavoury misogyny manifests itself in the treatment of Debussy's first serious partner, Gabrielle Dupont (Gaby), whom he describes as a 'well-dressed tart' (p. 71), and Lilly, who was 'losing her undeniable physical charms that had been her chief ornament' (p. 125)!
8 *Letters*, pp. 147–8.
9 BN Rés Vmf ms 53. Lesure, who quotes a small portion, agrees that it may have been prepared as an *aide-mémoire* for the ensuing divorce action; *Claude Debussy avant Pelléas ou les années symbolistes* (Langres, 1992), p. 163.
10 *Letters*, pp. 147–8.
11 Nichols, *Debussy Remembered*, p. 74.
12 I have been unable to find much information about this institution, but it seems to have been a private clinic in a building dating from 1902 or 1903 that had not been constructed for any specific purpose. The *Liste électorale* lists one Dr Robert Chancerel as a resident, also M. et Mme Nocard (I am indebted to Ruth Rennie for rooting out this information). Reading between the lines of Debussy's commentary, it is possible that 33, rue Blanche was an institution for women suffering from 'hysteria', a popular 'disorder' at the time.
13 Nichols, *Debussy Remembered*, pp. 77–9.
14 A neighbouring entry in the notebook (ms 53) noting the telephone number of 33, rue Blanche enables us to date this as around the middle of October 1904. Composition sketches for 'Jeux de vagues' are on the following page (see chapter 2).
15 See Lesure, *Avant Pelléas*, pp. 161–71.
16 Victor Seroff devotes several pages of his controversial biography to Debussy's marriages, and Bataille's play is quoted at length. See the chapter 'Day of judgement', pp. 241–55.
17 *Letters*, pp. 150–4.

18 Dietschy, *A Portrait*, p. 139.
19 The evidence is complicated by the fact that Debussy worked from both ends of the notebook (the pagination provided starts at the wrong end). The sentence alleging Lilly's infidelity precedes sketches for *La mer* at one end; the commentary, various jottings, and addresses precede one final sketch for *La mer* and two for *Le roi Lear* at the other. See pp. 13–14 for discussion of the nature of these sketches.
20 *A Portrait*, p. 128.
21 *Letters*, pp. 138–9.
22 *Debussy: Orchestral Music*, p. 24.
23 To Gabriel Pierné, 22 October 1907; *Letters*, p. 185.
24 *Debussy in Proportion*, pp. 132–3.

2 Genesis

1 *Debussy: His Life and Mind*, vol. 2, p. 27.
2 Letter to Suarès, *Cahiers Romain Rolland* 5, p. 206.
3 Discovered in the library of the Société d'Histoire et d'Archéologie de Saint-Malo. Spence is quoting Petit, who in his turn based his information on the reminiscences of an elderly canon, a Breton writer (Roger Vercel), and other, unspecified people. 'Debussy at sea', pp. 641–2.
4 *Letters*, p. 137.
5 *Debussy on Music*, p. 205.
6 *Letters*, p. 141.
7 8 October 1907; *Debussy Remembered*, p. 143.
8 'Allocution', *Revue Musicale*, special issue 'Claude Debussy 1862–1962', p. 147.
9 Rolf, 'Debussy's *La mer*', pp. 35–7.
10 Ibid. p. 202.
11 BN Rés Vmf ms 53.
12 In Rolf, 'Debussy's *La mer*', p. 300.
13 Letters dated 13 January and February 1905; *Lettres à son editeur*, pp. 24–5.
14 Ibid. p. 23.
15 Ibid. p. 24.
16 Ibid. p. 25.
17 Letter dated July 1904 and written from the Grand Hotel, Jersey, where Debussy was staying with Emma; *Letters*, p. 148.
18 Lesure remarks in his notes accompanying the Jersey letter that the phrase 'A la petite mienne' recalls a poem by Jules Laforgue, *Ô géraniums diaphanes*: 'Ô ma petite mienne, ô ma quotidienne'. *Correspondance*, p. 194.
19 Boulez's oft-expressed concern for accuracy in textual matters is not always borne out in practice, and certainly not in his CBS recording of *La mer*.
20 Rolf suggests that the only part of the opera remotely like *La mer* is near the end of Act I. 'Debussy's *La mer*', p. 53.
21 Example from British Library copy of 1905 edition with autograph revisions, BL K.5.d.16.
22 20 September 1952, unpublished letter.
23 Table 1 on p. 30 shows the range of variation between conductors.
24 *Œuvres complètes*, unpublished at time of writing.

3 *La mer* in performance

1 *Lettres à son editeur*, p. 15.
2 Seroff, *Debussy*, p. 234.
3 *Douze chefs d'orchestre* (Paris, 1924), p. 21.
4 *Debussy on Music*, pp. 30, 14.

5 Letters to Raoul Bardac and Durand; *Letters*, pp. 164, 162–3.
6 *Douze chefs*, p. 21.
7 Letters dated Saturday, 16 March 1905, and Saturday, 30 September 1905; *Lettres à son editeur*, pp. 26, 35.
8 Letter to Rolf in Nichols, *Debussy Remembered*, p. 183.
9 Dietschy, *A Portrait*, p. 139.
10 *La musique retrouvée, 1902–27* (Paris, 1928), pp. 146–7.
11 *Lettres à son editeur*, p. 39.
12 *Letters*, p. 186.
13 'Allocution', p. 150.
14 From *F-Pn* [Bibliothèque Nationale] Rés. Vm. Dos. 13 (19), entries for 20 and 25 January 1908. In Orledge, *Debussy and the Theatre* (Cambridge, 1982), p. 298.
15 Rolf, 'Debussy's *La mer*', p. 27.
16 Lawrence Gilman, *Harper's Weekly*, 3 March 1907; Philip Hale, *Boston Herald*, 3 March 1907. These and many other critical reactions are in Rolf, 'Debussy's *La mer*', pp. 313–43.
17 *Toscanini and Great Music* (London, 1939), pp. 165–8, 152.
18 '*La mer* par Claude Achille Debussy', *La Revue Musicale* (70, 1936), p. 118.
19 *Guide du concert* (1920–1).
20 *Le Temps* (24 October 1905), given in Vallas, *Claude Debussy*, p. 172.
21 Wednesday, 25 October 1905; *Letters*, pp. 163–4.
22 *La liberté*, given in Vallas, p. 173.
23 Recalled by Lawrence Gilman in *Toscanini and Great Music*, p. 151.
24 Quoted in Rolf, 'Debussy's *La mer*', pp. 323–4.
25 In Vallas, *Claude Debussy*, p. 174.
26 *The Maestro Myth: Great Conductors in Pursuit of Power* (London, 1991), p. 31.
27 Gramophone DB 4874–6, reissued on Vogue 665001 (CD). Two bars are missing in this recording: III/157–8.
28 For an incomplete but useful discography of *La mer* and other works up to the tape era (*c.* 1950), see M. G. Cobb, *Discographie de l'œuvre de Claude Debussy* (Geneva, 1975). Full discographies appear regularly in *Cahiers Debussy*.
29 Principal voice, secondary voice.
30 Lebrecht, *The Maestro Myth*, p. 75.
31 'Des fautes de copie à l'interprétation', p. 15.

4 The '*invisible* sentiments of nature'

1 *Debussy on Music*, p. 14.
2 See Christopher Palmer, *Impressionism in Music* (London, 1973).
3 Debussy arranged the *Der fliegende Holländer* overture for two pianos, four hands (published in 1890 by Durand et Schoenewerk).
4 As Gilson regretfully remarks in his autobiography, his *La mer* did not remain in favour for long. Only the second movement is currently available on CD (Marco Polo 8 2234 18).
5 Among several outstanding studies related to this subject the following are recommended: Stefan Jarocinski, *Impressionism and Symbolism*; Edward Lockspeiser, *Music and Painting*; Palmer, *Impressionism in Music*.
6 *His Life and Mind*, vol. 2, pp. 28–9.
7 Jarocinski, *Impressionism and Symbolism*, p. 161.
8 *His Life and Mind*, vol. 2, p. 232.
9 I am not sure that any original composer ever precisely followed a prescribed system of harmony. Nevertheless, by the end of the nineteenth century, harmonic practice was well codified, and there were those, like d'Indy, who would regard certain principles as inviolate.
10 'Impressionism', *New Grove*.

11 John House, *Monet: Nature into Art* (New Haven, 1986), pp. 25–6. See also Emmanuel Bondeville, 'Claude Monet–Claude Debussy', in *Aspects of Monet: a Symposium on the Artist's Life and Times*, ed. John Rewald and Frances Weitzenhoffer (New York, 1984).

12 Musée d'Orsay, Paris.

13 Letter to Durand, March 1908; *Letters*, p. 188. Peter's anecdote of Debussy at sea (see chapter 1) throws up an oft-cited parallel to an experience of Turner's, one that led to the greatest of his seascapes, *The Snowstorm*. In order to experience the storm to the full, Turner had himself lashed to a ship's mast, risking possible death (1842). Sadly, this anecdote is now thought to be part of mythology.

14 *His Life and Mind*, vol. 2, p. 26.

15 *Debussy on Music*, pp. 117–18.

16 Ibid. p. 233.

17 *Impressionism and Symbolism*, p. 133.

18 Evidence of Debussy's whimsical fondness for euphonious sounding names is provided in a different context: early in 1900 he told his friend Robert Godet about his marriage to Lilly Texier who had 'exchanged her inharmonious name for that of Lilly Debussy, much more euphonious as I'm sure everybody will agree'. *Letters*, p. 109.

19 Rolf, 'Mauclair and Debussy', pp. 13–23. For many years this story could not be found, its publication having been attributed to 27 instead of 26 February, *L'echo de Paris littéraire illustrée* (57, 1893).

20 Oscar Thompson, *Debussy: Man and Artist* (New York, 1937), pp. 324–5.

21 *Lettres à son editeur*, p. 23.

22 *Impressionism and Symbolism*, pp. 155–6.

23 The manuscripts entitled 'Etudes pour Fall H.U.' are housed in the Bibliothèque Nationale, Paris, ms 9885 BN.

24 Debussy's sketches are quite modest in their extent; nevertheless, there are two attempted completions of the opera, by Juan Allende Blin and Carolyn Abbate. Blin's has been recorded and is available on EMI CDM 7 64687 2.

5 Genre and style

1 Richard Langham Smith, notes accompanying EMI CD CDM 7 64364 2.

2 *Debussy on Music*, p. 16.

3 Ibid. p. 147.

4 Nichols, *Debussy Remembered*, p. 48.

5 *Letters*, p. 164.

6 Debussy was sympathetic to Schumann's music. See Howat, *Debussy in Proportion*, p. 133.

7 Martin Cooper, *French Music* (London, 1951), p. 159.

8 On at least one occasion Debussy referred to *La mer* as 'my symphony' (interview for *Azest*, incorrectly given as 'my symphonic poem' in *Debussy on Music*, p. 241), though he also called it 'symphonic sketches'. The English critic Ernest Newman described *La mer* as an 'orchestral suite' in *The Musical Times* (59, 1918), p. 343.

9 First Paris performance was on 5 March 1899.

10 Rolf, 'Debussy's *La mer*', p. 11.

11 *Debussy on Music*, p. 36.

6 Design

1 'Composition with twelve tones (1)', in *Style and Idea* (London, 1975), p. 216.

2 William Austin (ed.), *Debussy: Prelude to 'The Afternoon of a Faun'* (London, 1970), p. 71.

3 Richard Parks describes 'De l'aube à midi sur la mer' as an example of 'kinetic form' that 'evokes a locomotive conception of form as fluid and actively changing during a composition's

course'. This is opposed to 'morphological form' which is 'fixed and static'. *The Music of Claude Debussy*, p. 234.

4 'Debussy's "Jeux"', trans. Leo Black, *Die Reihe* 5 (Bryn Mawr, 1959), pp. 4, 10ff.

5 Golden Section is 'the way of dividing a fixed length in two so that the ratio of the shorter portion to the longer portion equals the ratio of the longer portion to the entire length . . . it approximates to 0.618034 (a little under two-thirds)'; *Debussy in Proportion*, p. 2. For Howat's extensive analysis of *La mer* see pp. 64–135.

6 Ansermet, *Ecrits* (Paris, 1962), p. 206.

7 Barraqué, *Debussy* (Paris, 1962), p. 89.

8 I am grateful to Julian Rushton for pointing this out. Another possibility is that Satie was joking.

9 I have chosen this recording, not because I consider it the most accurate or persuasive – I do not, but because it is widely available and has often been recommended as the best available version in publications such as *The Penguin Guide to Compact Discs*.

10 *Debussy: Orchestral Music*, p. 27.

11 Laloy, review of the first performance in *Mercure musical* (1 November 1905), p. 488.

12 See Howat, *Debussy in Proportion*, p. 74.

13 The tritone C–F♯, first heard in 1/8, is ubiquitous in *La mer*. Its structural function, except as a connective, is unclear. The same tritone is heard in many other works, including the operas *Rodrigue et Chimène* and *Pelléas et Mélisande*.

14 A pitch or chord only operates as a dominant if certain conditions are met. Through much of *La mer* they are not, so it is unhelpful to attempt to force musical events into traditional garments they ill-fit.

15 Figure after Howat, *Debussy in Proportion*, p. 111. Howat's approach to proportional structures requires clear formal divisions. If he is right and Debussy did calculate lengths of sections on the basis of Golden Section, sectional divisions become crucial in the analysis of *La mer*.

16 Unpublished paper recalled by Rolf, 'Debussy's *La mer*', p. 157.

17 Quoted in Howat, *Debussy in Proportion*, p. 114.

18 Other analyses begin the last section at bar 225 on account of the *au Mouvt*. My reason for favouring bar 219 is the continuity of the bass line from here to the end, which results in the final assertion of a tonic triad. This final part is, ironically, a rare example in *La mer* of a formal division rendered ambiguous by overlapping functions.

19 Descriptions like this are redolent of a manner of critical writing that is now very unfashionable. If works like *La mer* are ever to be fully appreciated, rapprochement between current analytical bias and the old interpretative manner is more than desirable, it is essential.

20 I use 'sentence' in Schoenberg's sense where the immediate repetition of a motif (or phrase) does not lead to local closure (as in an antecedent–consequent group or 'period' as he calls it) but to development and finally a closing phrase. He cites the opening of Beethoven's Piano Sonata in F minor, Op. 2 No. 1, as an example. Debussy's structures are not strictly comparable, I admit; in particular, the notion of closure is far from straightforward given the shortage of cadential articulation. See Schoenberg, *Fundamentals of Musical Composition* (London, 1967), pp. 20ff.

21 Recalled by Rolf, 'Debussy's *La mer*', p. 175.

22 Model-and-sequence construction has been given special status by Schoenberg's famous opposition of it to developing variation in his comparison of the music of Wagner and Brahms ('Brahms the Progressive', in *Style and Idea*). His treatment of the subject was partly polemical in that he regarded model and sequence as the inferior technique: it involved repetition rather than variation or development. Debussy makes little use of either in the sense that Schoenberg understood them, but it is interesting to note the increased use of model and sequence in the finale of *La mer*, where regular phrase structures are sustained by various types of repetition to a far greater extent than in 'Jeux de vagues'.

23 Quoted in Rolf, 'Debussy's *La mer*', p. 219.

24 *Debussy in Proportion*, p. 94.
25 Quoted in Nichols, *Debussy*, p. 92.
26 Poe, *A Descent into the Maelström* (1841).
27 Some conductors ignore this distinction, others like Reiner (RCA) use it as a pretext to thump the chorale chords very hard on their second appearance.

7 Material and 'immaterial' music

1 *Letters*, p. 184.
2 Ibid.
3 Terms such as 'phrase' and 'unit' mean different things to different people. My definition of phrase is the place taken up by the statement and immediate propagation of a motif. It will be separated from the next phrase by a new motivic start, a change in texture, or some other point of punctuation. A unit arises from two phrases that are closely associated. When two phrases become one phrase is hard to say. At some stage in the climax of 'Jeux de vagues' this change undoubtedly takes place, though clearly delineated two-bar subdivisions remain.
4 See chapter 6, n. 20.
5 Nichols, *Debussy Remembered*, p. 157.
6 See '*La Mer* de Debussy' for Barraqué's exhaustive analysis of *La mer* and clarification of what he meant by 'open forms'. Sadly, no English translation of this essay has appeared, and the problems posed by its translation probably mean that this will remain so. The posthumous publication of this essay is prefaced by a helpful introduction by Alain Poirier, 'L'histoire, "toujours recommencée" . . .', *Analyse musicale* (12, 1988), pp. 9–13.
7 In Françoise Gervais, 'La notion d'arabesque chez Debussy', *La revue musicale* (241, 1958), p. 14.
8 Ibid. p. 4.
9 See Julia d'Almendra, 'Debussy et le mouvement modal dans la musique du XXe siècle', in *Debussy et l'évolution de la musique au XXe siècle*, ed. Edith Weber (Paris, 1965), pp. 109–26.
10 Lockspeiser, *His Life and Mind*, vol. 1 (London, 1962), pp. 204–8.
11 *Debussy on Music*, p. 84.
12 Debussy was quite chameleon-like in the harmonic differences between works. 'The Little Shepherd' from *Children's Corner* (1906–8), for example, bases its two tonic cadences on an almost orthodox II^7–V–I progression with an identical version of the progression on the dominant in between.
13 The various manifestations of a tonic harmony suggest Schoenberg's array of 'transformations of . . . degrees in the tonic region', which show how a variety of chords can substitute for the tonic triad simply by semitonal changes or adding a seventh or ninth. *Structural Functions of Harmony* (London, 1954/69), p. 38.
14 The pointed A♭ in the trombones (bar 138) might be considered a conventional dominant were it not for the dissonant harmony sounding against it. In effect, this tenor A♭ is parenthetic, in no way detracting from the vigorously asserted bass B♭s of the previous bars.

Select bibliography

Barraqué, Jean. 'La Mer de Debussy, ou la naissance des formes ouvertes', posthumous publication of analytical notes, Analyse musicale (12, 1988), pp. 15–62

Cox, David. Debussy Orchestral Music, BBC Music Guides (London, 1974)

Debussy, Claude. Claude Debussy: Correspondance 1884–1918, selected and edited by François Lesure (Paris, 1993)

Debussy Letters, selected and edited by François Lesure and Roger Nichols, translated by Roger Nichols (London, 1987)

Debussy on Music, critical writings and interviews, collected and introduced by François Lesure, translated and edited by Richard Langham Smith (London, 1977)

Lettres de Claude Debussy à son editeur [Jacques Durand] (Paris, 1927)

Dietschy, Marcel. A Portrait of Claude Debussy, edited and translated by William Ashbrook and Margaret G. Cobb (Oxford, 1990)

Dömling, Wolfgang. Claude Debussy: 'La mer', Meisterwerk der Musik (Munich, 1976)

Goubault, Christian. Claude Debussy (Paris, 1986)

Gousset, Bruno. 'La prééminence du timbre dans le langage musical de La mer de Debussy', Analyse musicale (3, 1986), pp. 37–45

Howat, Roy. Debussy in Proportion: A Musical Analysis (Cambridge, 1983)

'Dramatic Shape in "Jeux de vagues", and its relationship to Pelléas, Jeux and other scores', Cahiers Debussy (new series 7, 1983), pp. 7–23

Jarocinski, Stefan. Impressionism and Symbolism, translated from the French by Rollo Myers (London, 1976)

Laloy, Louis. 'La mer', in Mercure et bulletin de la S.I.M. (Paris, 1908), pp. 209–14

Lockspeiser, Edward. Debussy et Edgar Poe (Monaco, 1962)

Debussy: His Life and Mind, vol. 2: 1902–18 (London, repr. Cambridge, 1978)

Music and Painting (London, 1973)

Monnard, Jean-François. 'Claude Debussy: "La Mer": Des fautes de copie à l'interprétation', Schweizerische Musikzeitung (121, 1981), pp. 11–16

Nichols, Roger (work-list by Robert Orledge). 'Claude Debussy', in The New Grove: Twentieth-Century French Masters (London, 1986), pp. 39–125

Debussy (London, 1972)

Debussy Remembered (London, 1992)

Parks, Richard S. *The Music of Claude Debussy* (New Haven, 1989)

Pommer, Max. Preface to Peters edition of *La mer* (Leipzig, 1972), pp. xvii–xxii

Rolf, Marie. 'Debussy's *La mer*: a critical analysis in the light of early sketches and editions', Ph.D. dissertation (University of Rochester, Eastman School of Music, 1976)

'Mauclair and Debussy: the decade from "Mer belle aux Iles Sanguinaires" to *La mer*', *Cahiers Debussy* (11, 1987), pp. 9–23

Seroff, Victor. *Debussy: Musician of France* (New York, 1956)

Spence, Keith. 'Debussy at sea', *The Musical Times* (120, 1979), pp. 640–2

Vallas, Léon. *Claude Debussy: His Life and Works*, translated by Maire and Grace O'Brien (Oxford, 1933)

Index

conducted by Toscanini 23, 28–9; dedication 15–16; deletion of fanfares 16–17; discarded movement titles 12, 14, 38–40; première in London 22–3; première in Paris 6, 21; premières in Boston and New York 23; recordings 27–31, 54, 97; rehearsals for première 20
other works: *Ariettes oubliées* 3; 'Ballet' 9; 'Ce qu'a vu le vent d'ouest' (*Préludes*, Book 1) 41; 'Colloque sentimental' 10; *La damoiselle élue* 19; *Danse sacrée et danse profane* 10; 'De grève' (*Proses Lyriques*) 1; *The Devil in the Belfry* 7; *D'un cahier d'esquisses* 9; 'En bateau' 1; *L'enfant prodigue* Lia's air 24; *Estampes* 9; *The Fall of the House of Usher* 7, 41–2, 44; *Fantaisie* for piano and orchestra 7, 34; 'Fêtes' 8–9; *Fêtes galantes* II 9, 15; 'Golliwog's cakewalk' (*Children's Corner*) 44; *Ibéria* 8, 9, 24; *Images* I 9; *Images* (orchestral) 9, 24; *L'isle joyeuse* 1, 2, 9; 'Jardins sous la pluie' 1; 'Le jet d'eau' (*Cinq poèmes de Baudelaire*) 1; *Jeux* 52; *King Lear* 10; *Masques* 9; 'La mer est plus belle' (*Trois mélodies*) 1; *Nocturnes* 6, 8–9, 16, 18–19, 24, 26, 47, 60; 'Nuages' 9; *Pelléas et Mélisande* 2–3, 5–6, 11, 16, 19, 23, 25, 38, 47, 49, 69, 96; *Petite suite* 1, 9; Piano Trio 7; Poe symphony 11, 41–2; *Prélude à l'après-midi d'un faune* 2, 6, 16, 22, 24, 47, 51–2; *Rapsodie* for saxophone and orchestra 10; 'Reflets dans l'eau' 1–2; *Rondes de printemps* 75; 'Sirènes' 1, 8–9; String Quartet 8, 24, 97; Symphony in B minor 7; *Trois chansons de France* 9
Debussy, Lilly (*née* Texier) 2–6, 41
Dieppe 3, 5, 14
Dietschy, Marcel 1, 6
Ducasse, Roger 10

Dukas, Paul 32
Durand (publishing house) xi, 6, 37
Durand, Jacques 5–6, 12–15, 19–20, 22, 40, 47

Eastbourne 6
Eimert, Herbert 52, 97
Epstein, David 82

Fauré, Gabriel 3
  La bonne chanson 3
Fontainas, André 85
Forte, Allen x, xii
Franck, César 26, 35, 45–50, 57
  Béatitude No. 4 21
  Piano Quintet 48
  Prélude, aria et finale in E major 47
  Prélude, choral et fugue in B minor 47

Garban, Lucien xii
Garden, Mary 3–4
Gervais, Françoise 85
Gilman, Lawrence 23, 26
Gilson, Paul 35–6
  La mer 33–5, 83
Glazunov, Alexander *The Sea* 33, 76
Golden Section x, 17, 53
Green, Douglass 61
Griffes, Charles *Pleasure Dome* 24

Hall, Elisa 10
Haydn, Franz Joseph 76
  Symphony in D ['London'] 21
Hokusai, Katsushika 'The hollow of the wave off Kanagawa' 37
House, John 37
Howat, Roy x, 9, 17, 52–3, 60–1, 68–9

Impressionism ix–x, 3, 30, 32, 35–8, 51, 96–7
Indy, Vincent d' 2, 8, 30, 35, 38, 45–7, 49, 53, 82
  Jour d'été à la montagne 38, 45–6
  Symphonie sur un chant montagnard français 7, 21
  Symphony No. 2 45, 47

Made in the USA
Middletown, DE
16 September 2018